HOW TO DRAW ANIME Characters

DRAW WITH MEI

HOW TO DRAW ANIME Characters

MEI YU

union square kids
NEW YORK

This book is dedicated to all of you who love drawing and anime, and to all you parents, teachers, and librarians who support children in art!

Union Square & Co., LLC, is a subsidiary of Sterling Publishing Co., Inc.

ISBN 978-1-4549-5909-0 (paperback)
ISBN 978-1-4549-5910-6 (ebook)

Library of Congress Control Number: 2025931431

For information about custom editions, special sales, and premium purchases, please contact specialsales@unionsquareandco.com.

Printed in Malaysia

Lot #:
2 4 6 8 10 9 7 5 3 1

06/25

unionsquareandco.com

Cover and interior design by Julie Robine

CONTENTS

Hi! I'm Mei Yu! Join me, and I'll show you how to draw all kinds of easy anime characters!

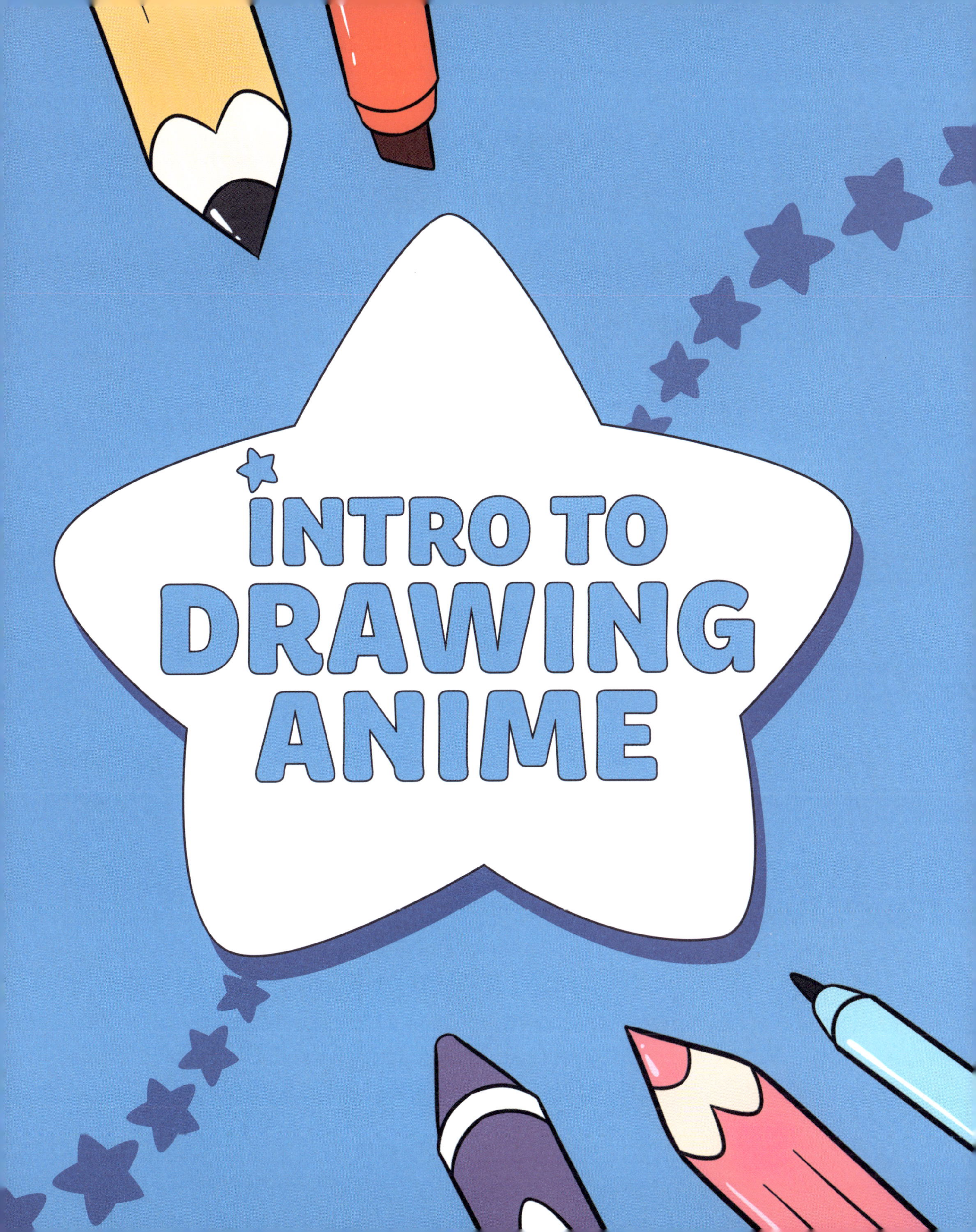
INTRO TO
DRAWING
ANIME

YOU CAN BE AN ANIME ARTIST!

WHAT IS ANIME?

You may have seen anime characters before, on TV, in card games, or as adorable plushies in your friend's room.

But wait—what is anime? And how can you create anime characters?

"Anime" is Japanese for "animation." Many fans around the world think of anime as Japanese animation and cartoons.

They can be epic fantasies, fun comedies, horror, action, or even about ordinary, daily lives.

Some popular types of anime characters include magical girls who fight evil, warriors from fantasy worlds, and cool villains.

They can have nice hair, stylish clothes, and memorable expressions.

You can learn how to draw some of them in this book!

There are many anime fans, including those who love to draw their own anime characters!

Are you one of them?

DIFFERENCES BETWEEN ANIME & CARTOON ART STYLES

✦ EYES:

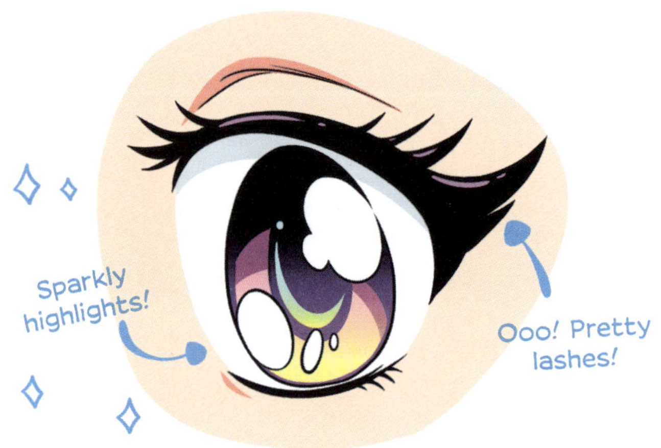

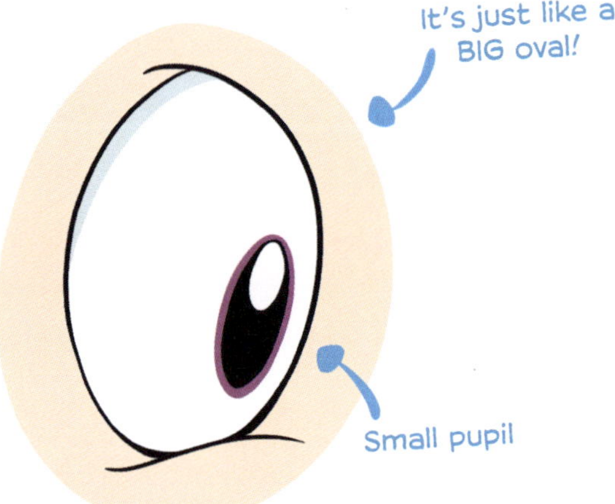

Anime
Eyes in anime tend to have large irises, with big, shiny highlights and shading.

Cartoons
Some eyes in cartoons can have a tiny pupil and lots of white space in the eye.

✦ NOSES & MOUTHS:

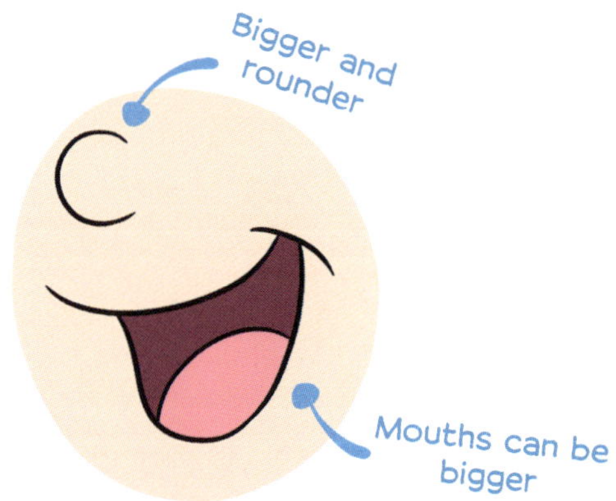

Anime
Anime noses tend to be small and pointy, with no nostrils. (Don't worry—they can still breathe! Somehow . . .) Smiling mouths are like triangles.

Cartoons
Noses in other art styles can be larger and rounder. Some can have nostrils. Mouths can be round and wide.

FACES:

Anime

Anime faces can have pointy chins, large eyes, and geometric shapes for hair.

Cartoons

Faces in other art styles can have rounded chins, softer hair, and exaggerated eyes.

BODIES:

Anime

Characters usually have more realistic proportions and normal-looking limbs.

Cartoons

Some characters in cartoons can have exaggerated or super-skinny limbs, large feet, and goofy hair!

WHAT TO USE

PENCILS

Pencils can be the easiest art tool to use! A good starting point is your school pencil or an HB pencil!

HB

COLORED PENCILS

Colored pencils, or pencil crayons, come in lots of colors! Press lightly on their leads so they don't break.

PENS

CRAYONS

MARKERS

GEL PENS

TEMPLATES

What are templates?

Templates are premade drawings of heads and bodies that you can draw right on top of to complete! This makes drawing faces and characters easier.

At the end of each lesson, you have a practice template, PLUS more templates at the end of each chapter for extra practice!

Here's a Head Template with face guidelines:

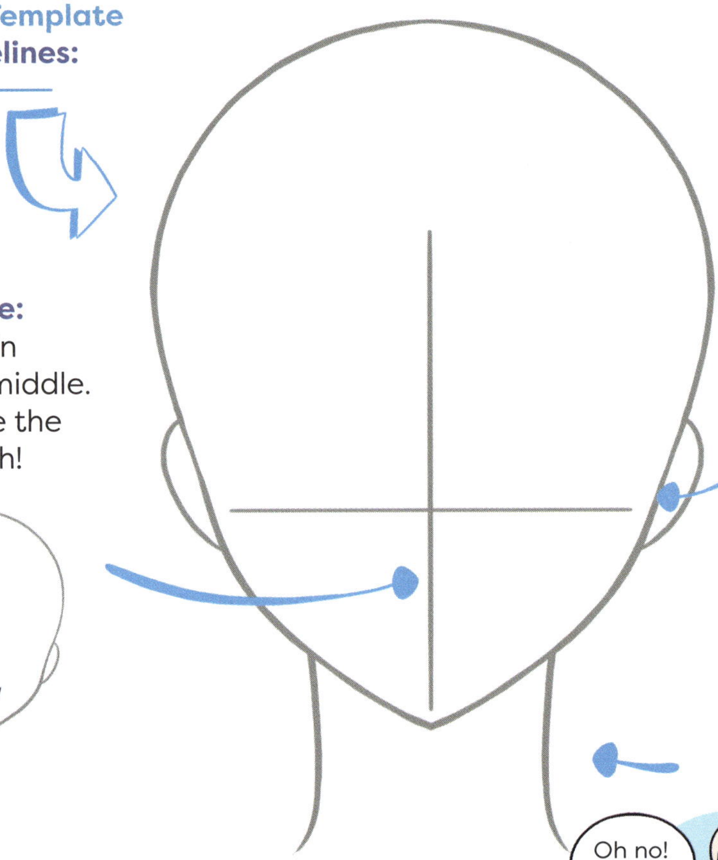

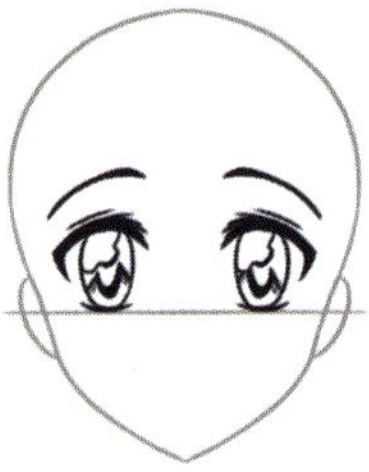

The Middle Line:
Splits the face in half down the middle. Helps you place the nose and mouth!

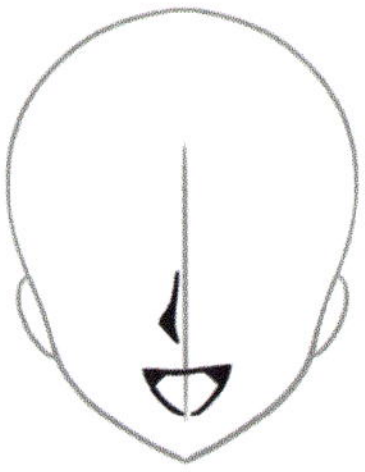

The Eye Guideline:
Helps you place the eyes on a face!

A Neck!
Nice to have one unless you want your character to be a floating head . . .

Here's a Body Template with guidelines!

Here's a full body template example. Note the line going through the middle of the body—similar to the face template's.

These guidelines help you place clothing on top of your character!

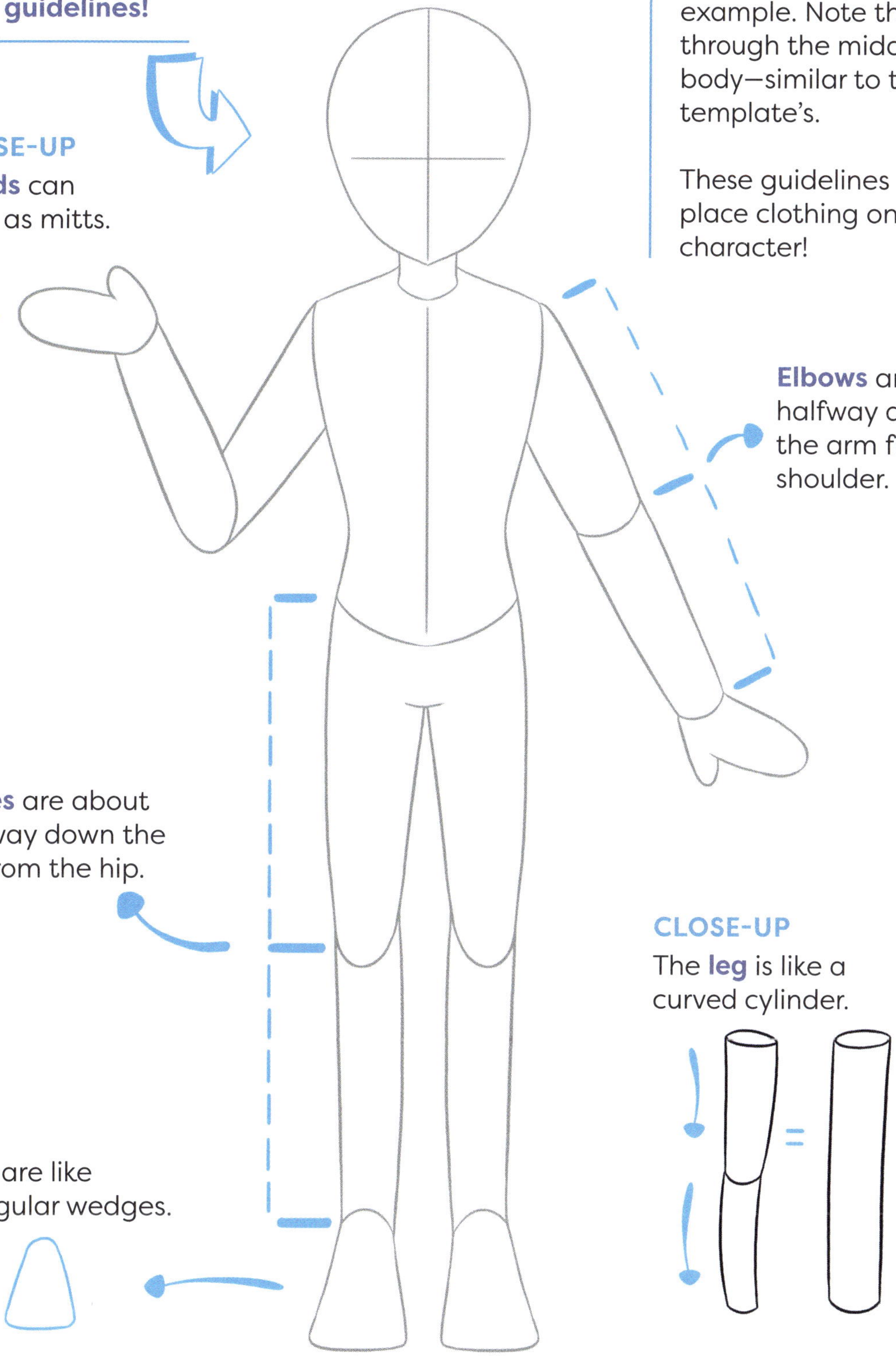

CLOSE-UP

Hands can start as mitts.

Elbows are about halfway down the arm from the shoulder.

Knees are about halfway down the leg from the hip.

CLOSE-UP

The **leg** is like a curved cylinder.

Feet are like triangular wedges.

HOW TO USE TEMPLATES

In this face template, the hair is already pre-drawn to make finishing the head easier.

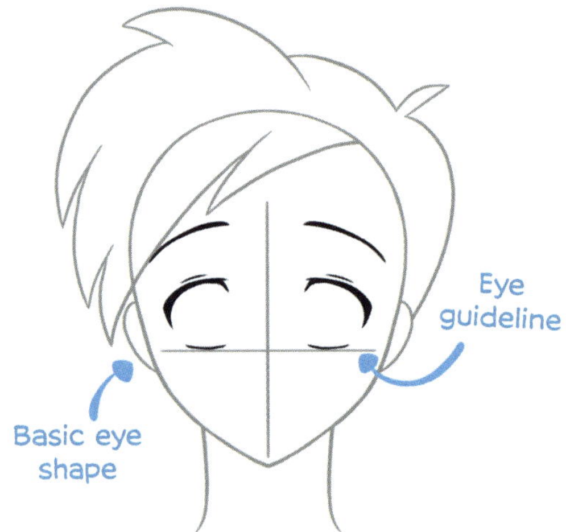

Use the horizontal eye guidelines to draw the eye shapes so they are even.

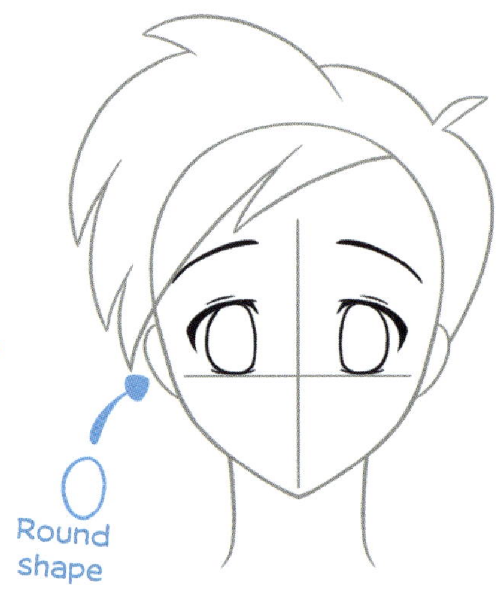

Fill in the oval eyes inside the shapes.

Use the face's middle line to draw the nose and mouth centered in the middle of the face.

Draw smaller ovals in the eyes for shiny highlights.

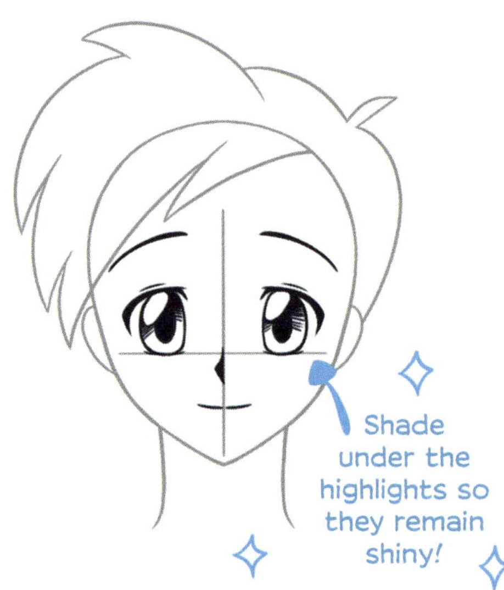

Add dark pupils in the eyes, under the shiny white highlights!

MIX IT UP!

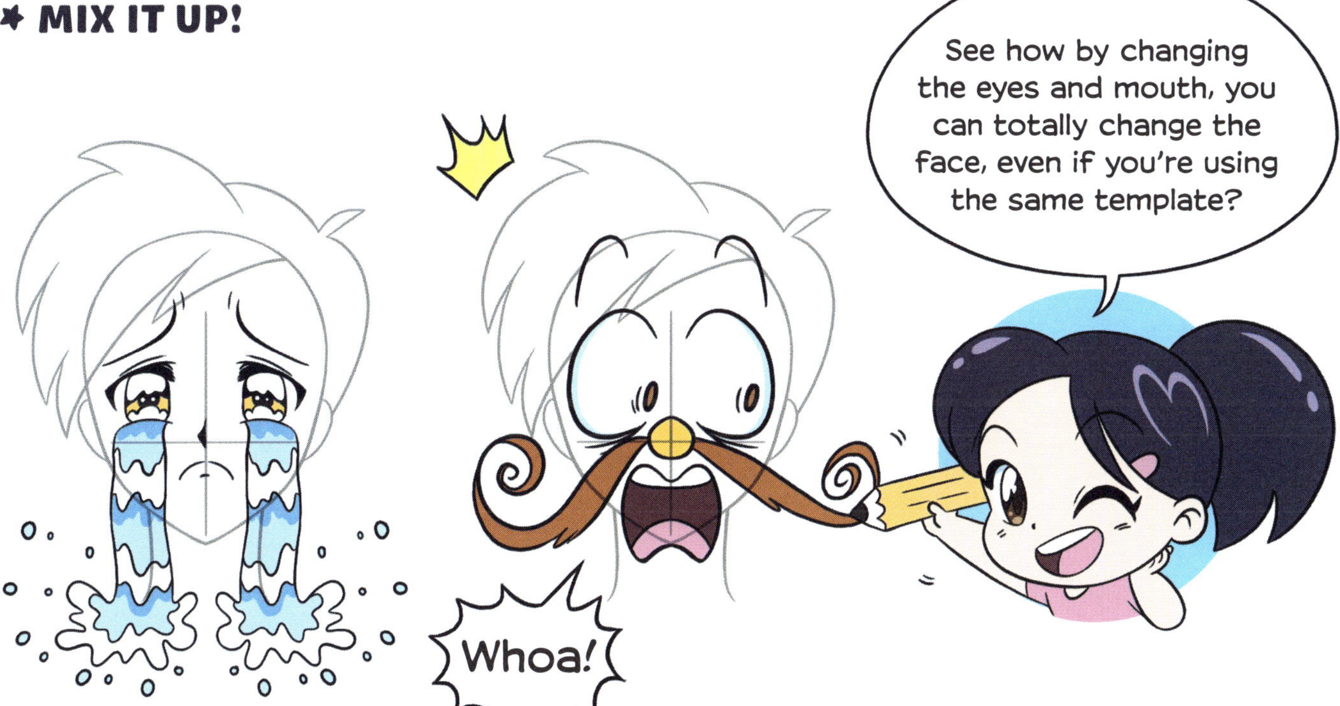

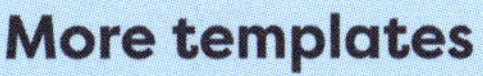

More templates

This book is packed with many different types of templates for you to practice and design your own faces, expressions, hair, outfits, and more!

POPULAR TYPES OF ANIME CHARACTERS

Before you begin, let's look at some types of characters that are common in anime!

THE SCHOOLGIRL

A staple in anime, the Schoolgirl is usually in traditional Japanese school uniforms with varying designs. She often wears either a sailor top or a blazer, with a skirt or pants.

THE COOL KID

The Cool Kid is outgoing and friendly. He is usually the main character or a major secondary character. His outfits are often casual, loose, and baggy.

THE VILLAIN

The Villain may be a stylish dresser, with a sinister but handsome face. His hairdo can be cool, wild, or jagged! His outfit may have sharp points to look dangerous.

THE PRINCESS

The Princess can be found in fairy-tale, fantasy, sci-fi, and romance anime. She's got a seemingly endless wardrobe of glam outfits. Her hairstyle is usually elegant or extravagant.

THE POWERFUL WARRIOR

The Powerful Warrior is popular in fantasy and action anime. He may have thicker muscles for lifting big, heavy swords, with cool armor for his outfit, and a scar or tattoo to stand out!

THE CAT GIRL

The Cat Girl is half-girl, half-cat. Her face is human, but she's got big cat ears sticking out! She may have smooth skin in various colors, or she may have fur.

COLORFUL COLORS!

Color choice is an important factor in deciding how your characters will look! Let's see how each color can affect a character design.

PRIMARY COLORS

There are three primary colors: red, yellow, and blue. These colors cannot be made by mixing any other colors. But, if you mix primary colors in different combinations, you can create any other color! Cool, huh?

RED
It's bright, attention getting, and intense! It can symbolize love, anger, heat, or danger.

Try reds on characters to make them a hothead, or angry or courageous, like this guy.

YELLOW
Yellow can represent sunshine, warmth, and happiness.

You can add yellow to characters to make them look energetic or cheerful, like her.

BLUE
Blue is a cool, calming color. It can also make a character look more icy, serene, or sad.

Try this for a calm, tranquil character, or someone who has a case of the blues, like him.

SECONDARY COLORS

Secondary colors are made when you mix two primary colors together, like these:

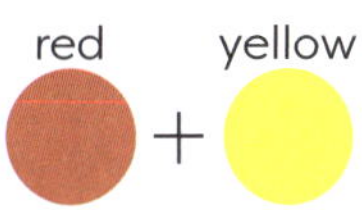

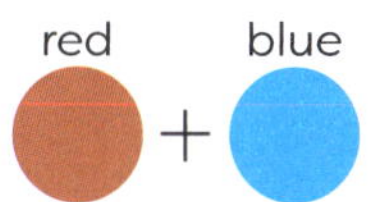

ORANGE
Orange is warm and energetic. It can help create a cozy "sunset" or "autumn" look for your characters, like this pumpkin lover.

GREEN
Green symbolizes life, nature, and renewal. But some characters could be "green with envy." It can also be used for villains like this.

VIOLET
This color can convey royalty, luxury, and wealth. You can also try violet for creative, mysterious, or magical characters, like this young wizard.

OTHERS

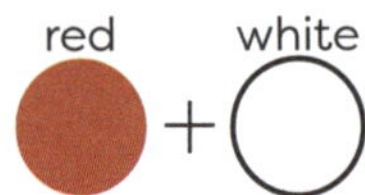

blue + yellow + red

PINK
Pink is a cute color to use for young, bubbly, or glam characters. Try using it for a magical girl, a popular girl at school, or a princess.

BROWN
Brown can be warm and grounded. It can give an "earthy" feel to any character. Try using browns for those who are reliable or mature.

BLACK
Black can be mixed with colors to make them darker. Try black on characters for classy, punk, or powerful looks.

WHITE
White can be mixed with colors to make them look lighter. Try white on characters for angelic or innocent looks.

THE COLOR WHEEL

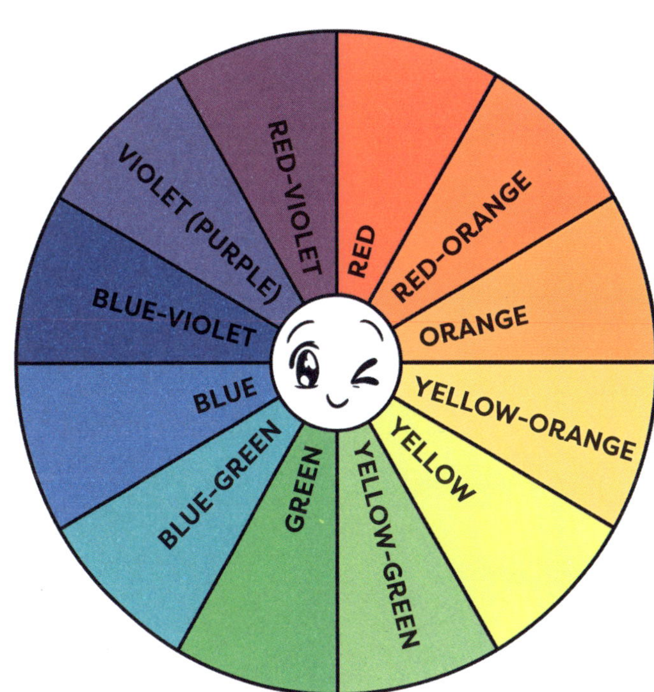

Color relationships

By grouping certain colors with other colors, you can create different effects:

Warm colors: red, orange, yellow

They can create feelings of warmth, coziness, or anger!

Cool colors: green, blue, violet

They can make you feel cool, calm, or sad!

Complementary colors

Colors opposite of each other on the color wheel can look striking together because they look very different from each other!

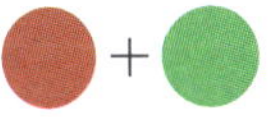  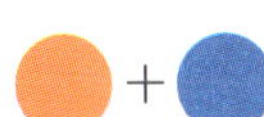

Analogous colors

These are colors beside each other on the color wheel. When placed together, they can look harmonious, like this.

Let's start with some easy step-by-step lessons on drawing anime heads and faces!
There are a lot of design choices to help you make different expressions!

1

HEADS AND EXPRESSIONS

FRONT HEAD

OMG! Let's have fun with these faces!

Here's our first art lesson, with this handy front head template! Don't worry about drawing the entire head—just jump right into drawing fun expressions!

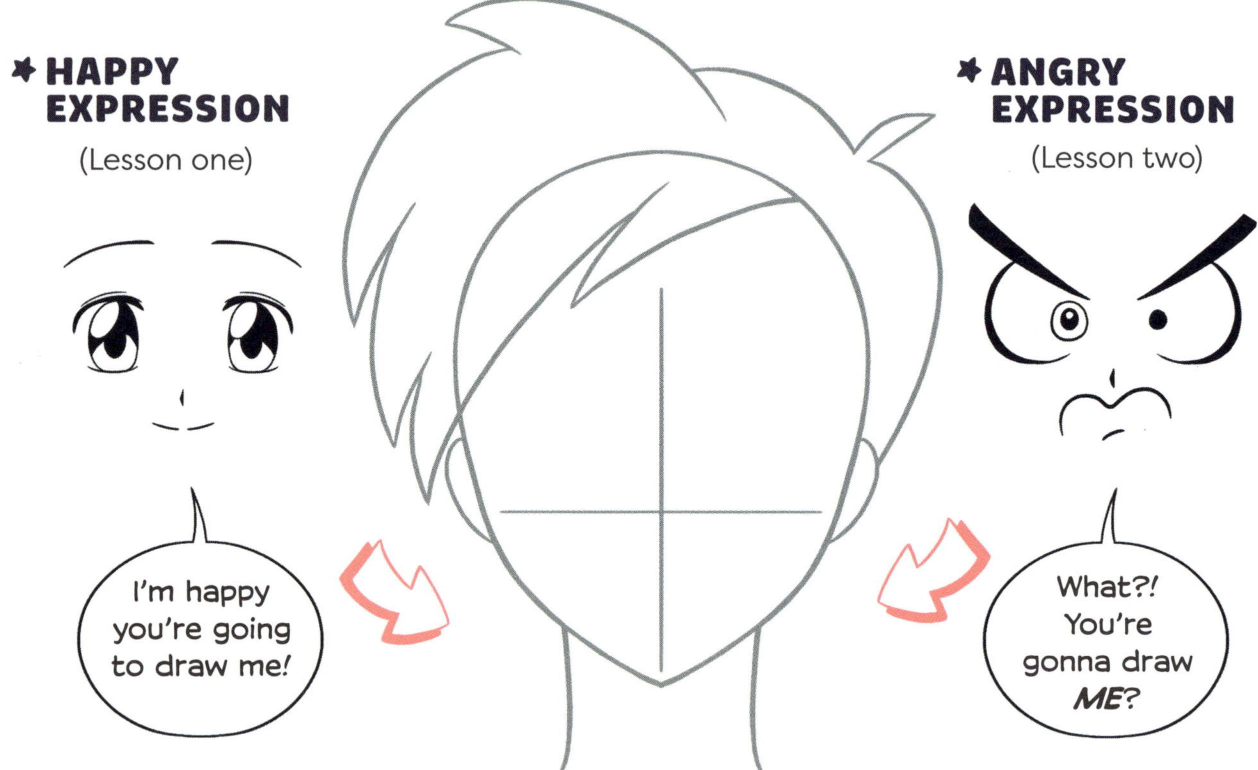

What face will this character have? It's up to you! Follow each lesson by using the head template at the end.

First, we'll learn how to draw these two expressions step by step. Then, use the skills you learned to create your own expressions on the template.

Note: This template has hair pre-drawn. We'll learn how to draw hair in the next chapter.

✦ LESSON ONE: HAPPY EXPRESSION

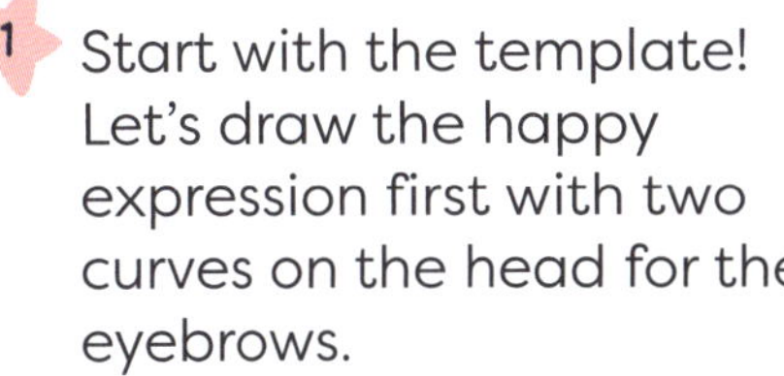

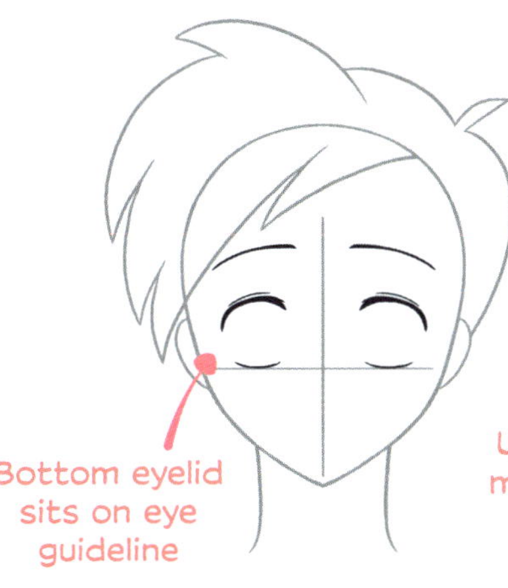

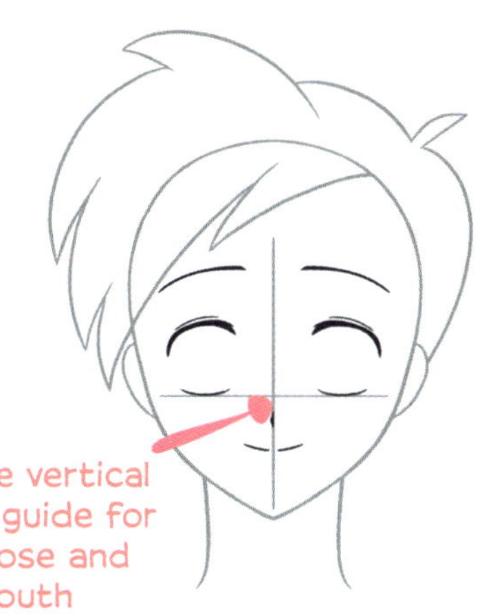

1 Start with the template! Let's draw the happy expression first with two curves on the head for the eyebrows.

2 Now use the face guidelines to help place the eye shapes.

3 Let's give him a nose and a smile!

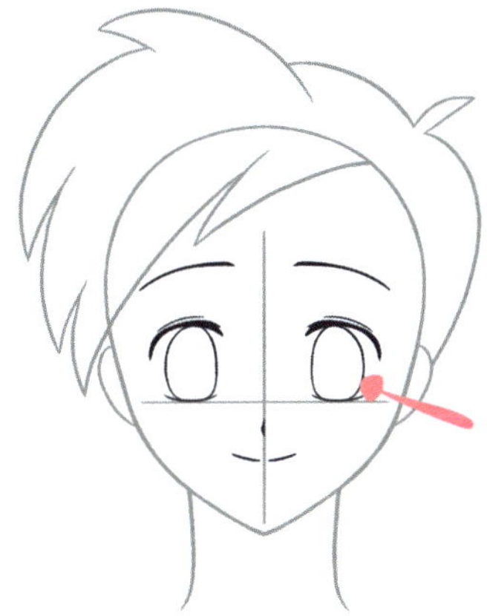

4 Draw ovals in the eyes for the irises.

5 Now draw an oval highlight in each iris to make them shiny!

6 Under each highlight, draw a dark oval pupil with a dark shadow on the top part of the irises.

The size of the white highlight in the eye will affect the look of the character.

Big highlight: friendly, alert, wide

Small highlight: can look less alert but still cute

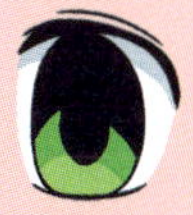

Eyes with just the dark pupil and no highlight can look intense or serious, or like the character is under a spell

LET'S COLOR!

1 Bring your character to life with colors! Start with the skin color on one side of the face.

2 Now color the whole face and neck. Leave some white around the eyes.

3 Color the hair, starting with the cool bangs.

4 Fill in the rest of the hair.

5 Lastly, color the eyes. He has a warm color palette with red hair and yellow eyes.

Try other colors for him! Instead of warm colors, try cool ones! He looks calm.

If you want him to look more punk or edgy, try dramatic black with bold streaks for his hairdo!

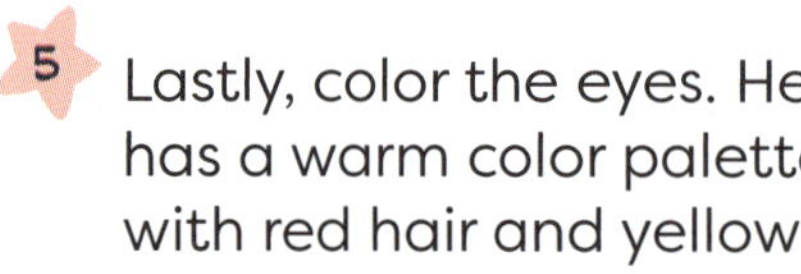

NOW YOU TRY!

Make a photocopy of this head template, then practice drawing expressions on it! Use the lessons in Chapter 1 to help you. There are more fun face ideas at the end of this chapter!

★ LESSON TWO: ANGRY EXPRESSION

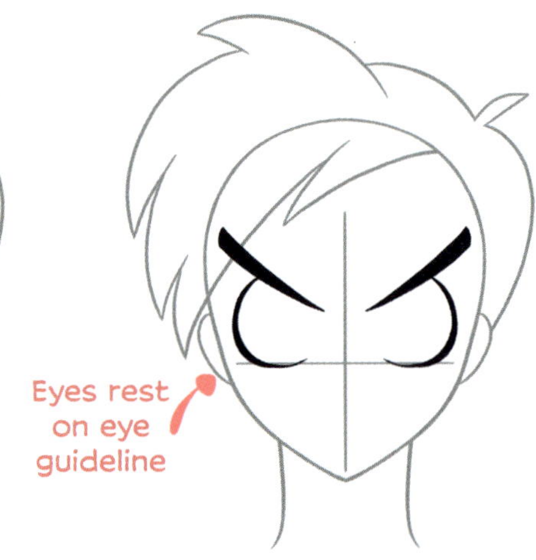

1 Here, we're starting with the same head template, but this time, we'll make him ***ANGRY!!!***

2 Start with some super-thick eyebrows! Both go down toward the vertical middle line.

3 What big eyes! Use the horizontal eye guideline to help you place them.

4 Yikes! Add tiny pupils with lots of white space around them to the eyes.

5 Use the vertical middle line to draw the nose and mouth.

There are many different ways to draw angry eyes. Try different thicknesses of eyebrows, various eye sizes, and pupil shapes!

Which will you choose?

Rectangle (for more serious characters)

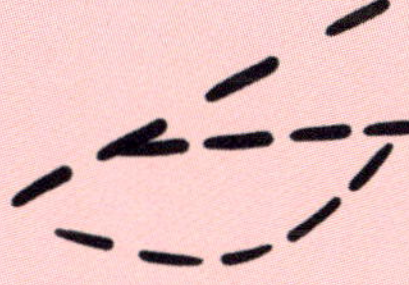

Round (for funny or cartoony characters)

ANIME SYMBOLS

Anime characters can magically sprout special symbols or icons on or near themselves when various expressions call for more emphasis.

Tense vein symbol: Add to characters' heads to indicate anger

Flames: Can be placed by mouths or ears

Funny steam clouds— wait! I'm not an airhead!

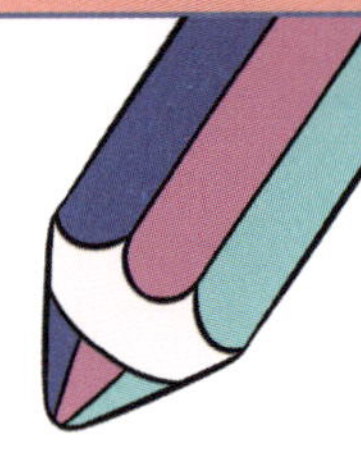

LET'S COLOR!

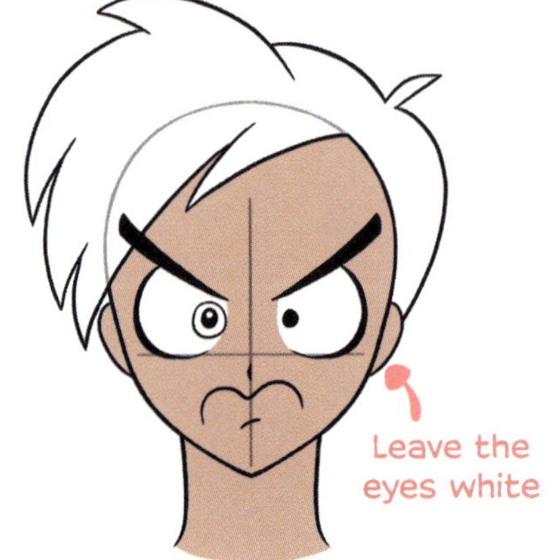

1. Give this angry boy colors! Start with the color on one side of the face.
2. Now color the whole face and neck.
3. Color the hair. Try a striking color that will stand out!

4. Fill in the rest of the hair.
5. Give his bigger pupil a bright color! Add white hair shine with a gel pen.

OTHER COLORS

Awww! Who's an adorable grumpy guy? Pink adds extra sweetness, which makes him ***angrier...***

You can also add greens to make him look seasick!

NOW YOU TRY!

Make a photocopy of this head template, then practice drawing expressions on it! Use the lessons in Chapter 1 to help you. There are more fun face ideas at the end of this chapter!

SIDE HEAD

Now that we know how to draw faces from the front view, let's use this side head template for drawing faces in profile!

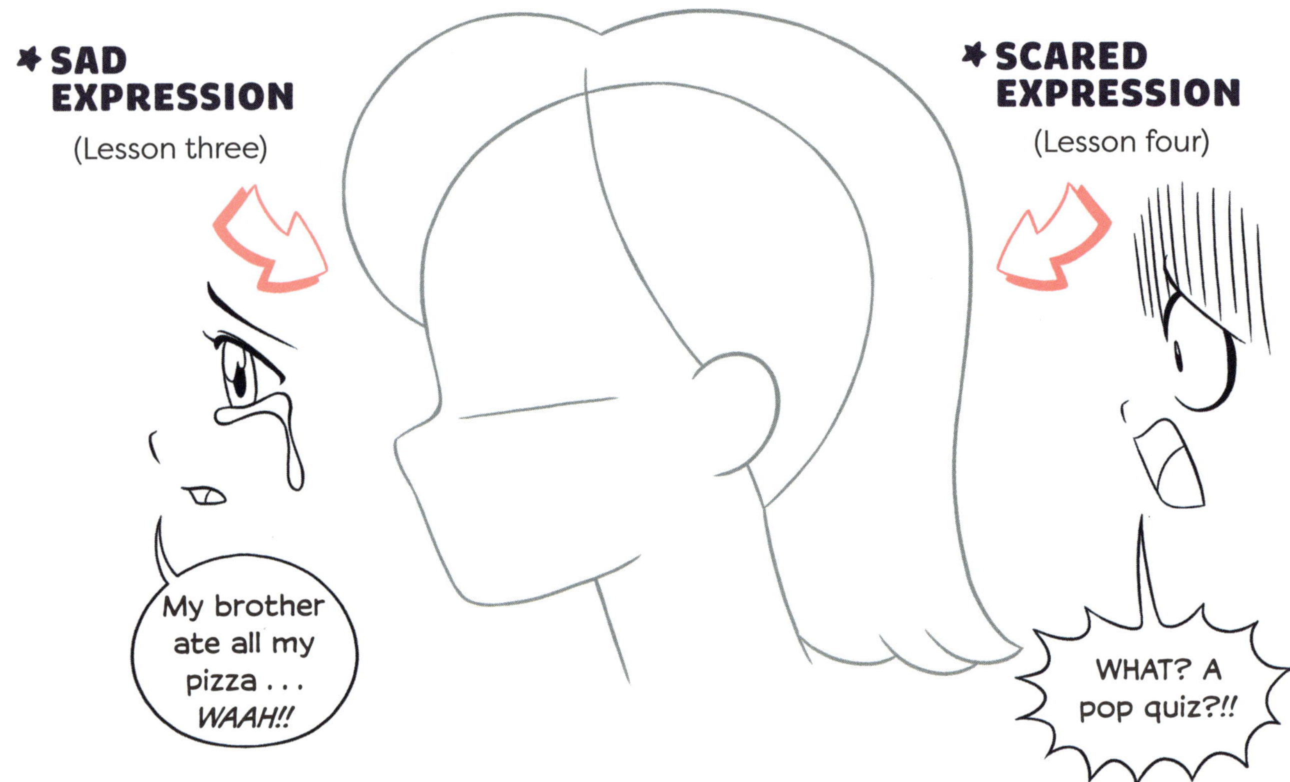

Let's draw these side view expressions by using the head template at the end. You'll get more face ideas at the end of this chapter, too.

First, we'll learn how to draw these two expressions step by step. Then, use the skills you learned to create your own expressions on the template.

✱ LESSON THREE: SAD EXPRESSION

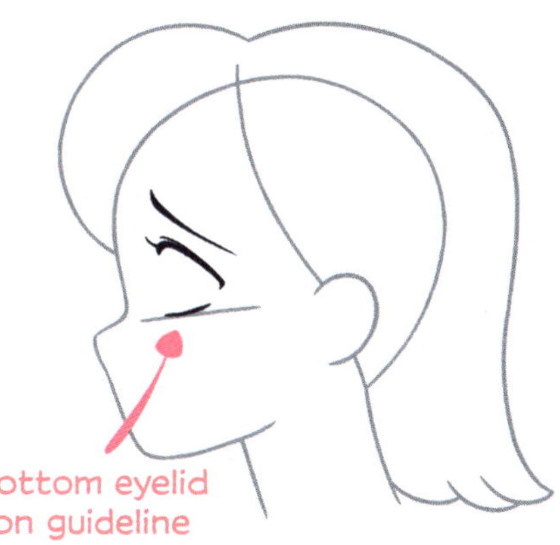

1. Start with the template! Let's draw the sad expression first!
2. Draw a tilted eyebrow high above the eye guideline.
3. Use the eye guideline to help you draw the basic eye shape.

Anime mouths can go on one side of the face!

4. Draw tears along the bottom eyelid, with a drop coming down.
5. Draw a squished oval for the iris, with a wiggly highlight.
6. Add a dark pupil under the highlight. Then, draw a small, curved mouth.

Here are some other fun ways to draw tears for sad characters:

Small and dainty, at the eye corner

A fun, exaggerated, cartoony look!

LET'S COLOR!

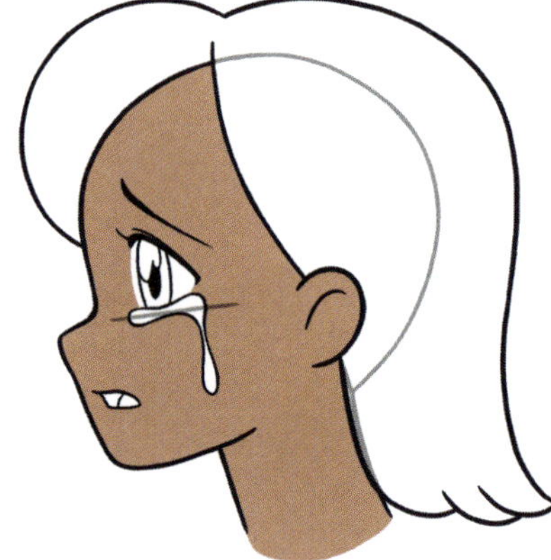

1 Choose a skin color first. Color along the edges, then go inward.

2 Fill in the face and neck with the skin color. Leave the eye area white.

3 For fun, I'm coloring her hair a cool blue, because she's got "the blues."

Use a white gel pen for hair highlights!

4 Now color her tears a light blue, and her eyes.

I made her eyes yellow so they stand out from the blue tears!

Try dark hair with bright streaks for a youthful, punk, or emo look.

You can make her look like a pretty fantasy or alien character with unusual skin and hair color combos!

NOW YOU TRY!

Make a photocopy of this head template, then practice drawing expressions on it! Use the lessons in Chapter 1 to help you. There are more fun face ideas at the end of this chapter!

✦ LESSON FOUR: SCARED EXPRESSION

1 Start with her scared eyebrow tilting high above the horizontal eye guideline.

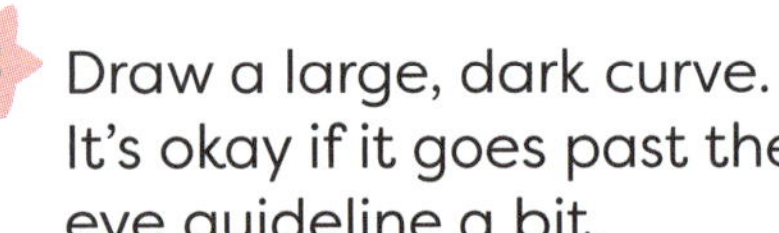

2 Draw a large, dark curve. It's okay if it goes past the eye guideline a bit.

3 Now draw a tiny pupil. For scared expressions, tiny pupils are effective.

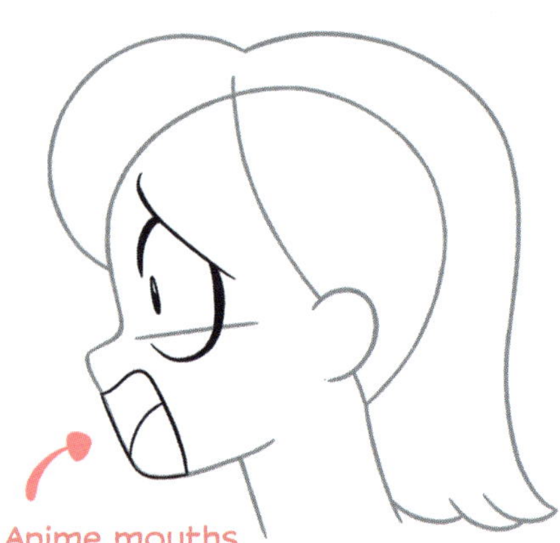

Anime mouths can often cover the chin area!

4 Make the open mouth BIG!! Drop it down to the chin line of the face template.

Here are more fun ways to draw a scared face!

You don't have to draw the pupil. Leave the eye white for a terrified look.

Try dropping the mouth past the chin. She's experiencing an eye-opening moment!

Which one will you choose?

5 A great way to make anime characters look scared or worried is to draw lots of dark vertical lines on their faces.

6 To emphasize her fear, add some sweat drops flying from her head!

ANIME SWEAT DROPS

You can use different sweat drops for anime characters to show their different moods. Here are other examples:

Small sweat drops around the head are good for scared or embarrassed characters!

A classic sweat drop! Place on the heads of characters who are unamused, nervous, embarrassed, or bored.

LET'S COLOR!

1 Choose a skin color first. Color along the edges, then go inward.

2 Fill in the face and neck with the skin color. Leave the eye area white.

3 Start coloring the hair along the edges, then move downward.

4 Color the rest of her hair.

5 Color the sweat drops, mouth, and blue scared lines!

OTHER COLORS

Try drawing blue lines on top of her hair and color the top half of her face blue to create more fear!

If you want dark, shiny hair, use a gel pen to draw squiggly white highlights!

NOW YOU TRY!

Make a photocopy of this head template, then practice drawing expressions on it! Use the lessons in Chapter 1 to help you. There are more fun face ideas at the end of this chapter!

BONUS IDEAS

Yay! You're done with Chapter 1! Here are fun face ideas you can try on the templates!

Determined eyes

Mischievous smirk

He's up to something . . . watch out!

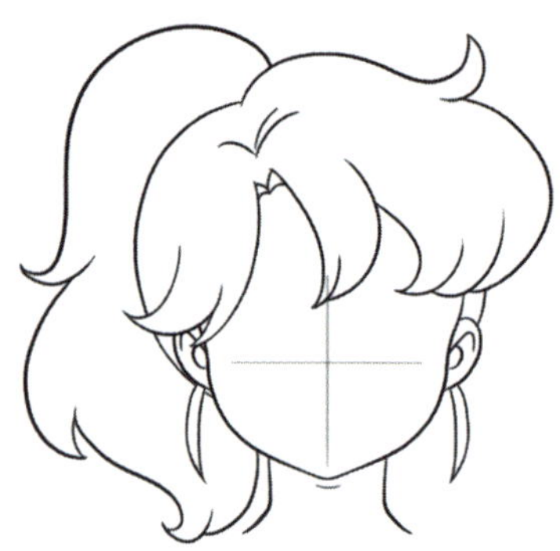

Big, cute eyes with large highlights and blushy cheeks

Cute mouth that can resemble an animal's

Aww! Puppy eyes

Tiny pupils in large eyes, with tense eyebrows and sweat drops

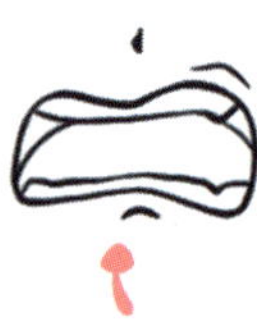

Big, wide mouth

Oh no!! He stepped in something!

Intense, closed eye with bold eyebrow

Cheek curve hides mouth line, and tongue sticks out

Funny sound effect! Did he just get grounded?

Eye wide with energy and gentle blush lines on cheek

Rounded triangle for mouth

Anime mouths can be on one side of face in side views

Tilted eyebrow on top of eye can make it look tense

Small, open snarl

Uh-oh, her brother just read her diary!

EXTRA TEMPLATES

You can photocopy these to practice as much as you want!

Here are extra head templates from Chapter 1 for you to practice drawing faces!

Now let's learn how to draw hairstyles for different faces step by step!
You can also see how different colors and shapes of hairstyles can affect various character designs!

2

HAIRSTYLES

FRONT HAIR

Let's give this guy cool hairdos with the help of this front head template! The face is already drawn, so let's focus on creating stylish 'dos!

✱ SPIKY HAIR

(Lesson one)

✱ FLOPPY HAIR

(Lesson two)

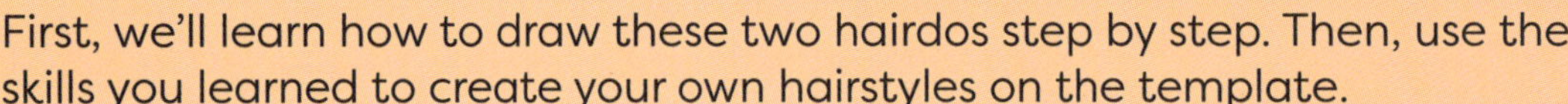

Get your comb and scissors, er, *pencil and eraser*, ready! You decide which hairstyle this character can have! Follow each lesson by using the face template at the end.

First, we'll learn how to draw these two hairdos step by step. Then, use the skills you learned to create your own hairstyles on the template.

Note: Templates in this chapter have pre-drawn faces. Learn how to draw faces in the previous chapter.

✦ LESSON ONE: SPIKY HAIR

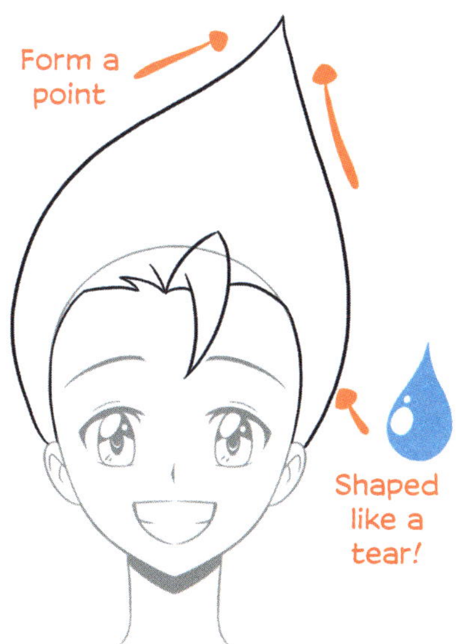

1 Start with a piece of hair in the middle of the template's forehead.

2 Draw two curves from the middle piece of hair around the face.

3 Draw the main shape of the hair first. We'll use this basic shape to help with the spikes next.

4 Draw spikes as zigzags inside the big teardrop shape for the hair spikes. They point toward the top.

5 Now erase the extra lines inside the teardrop shape so only the spikes remain.

★ LET'S COLOR!

1. Add more personality with colors! Start with the skin color on one side of the face.
2. Color the whole face and neck.
3. Choose a color for his hair. Start on one side.

4. Color in the rest of his hairdo! He's a grass-head.
5. Make his eyes stand out with colors! Use a white gel pen for wavy hair highlights.

OTHER COLORS

Use natural hair colors if you want your character to be less flashy and more realistic.

Try other bold colors for his hair. Red can make him look excitable, lively, or loud.

NOW YOU TRY!

Make a photocopy of this head template, then practice drawing hairstyles on it! Use the lessons in Chapter 2 to help you. There are more fun hair ideas at the end of this chapter!

✱ LESSON TWO: FLOPPY HAIR

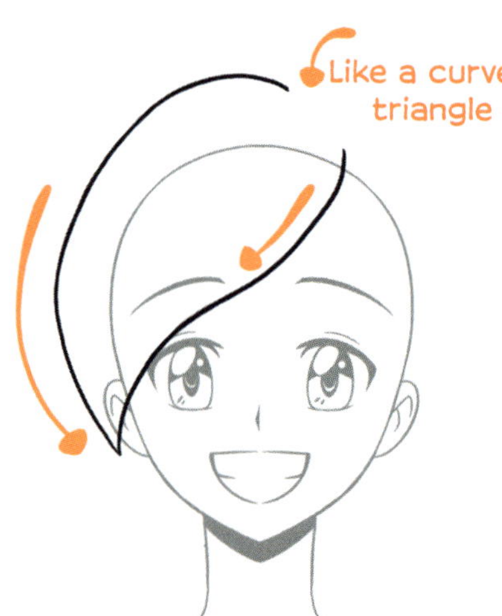

1. Using the same head template, let's make his hair flop down this time.
2. Start by drawing the basic shape of his bangs on one side.
3. Now draw the other side of the hair that curves along the head.

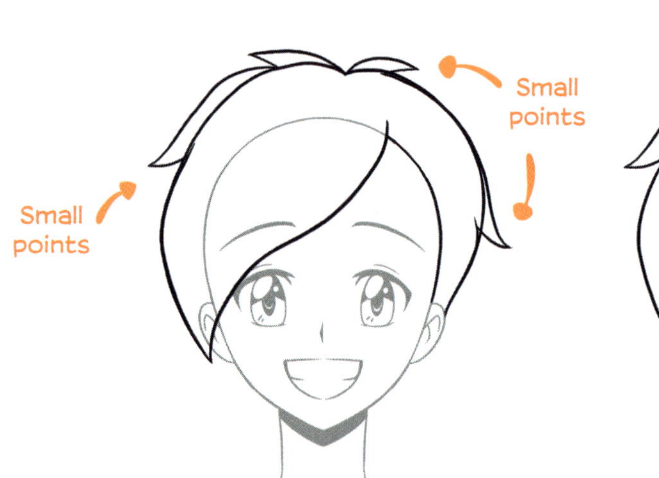

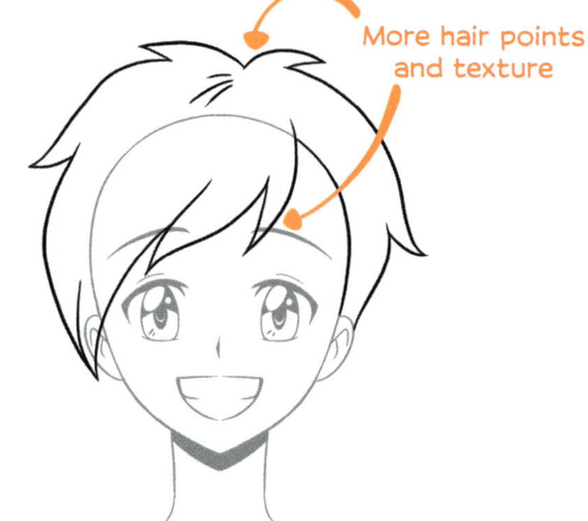

4. Add details by drawing small points sticking out of the hair's basic shape.
5. Draw more points of hair coming out of the bangs by the face.

Make your character look different just by changing how you draw the shapes and length of their hair!

HAIR SHAPES

Stiff, jagged hair

Most lines are straight and stiff, not curved. Try this for energetic or brash characters.

Soft, fluffy hair

Hair lines are soft and curved. This can make someone look friendly or bubbly.

HAIR LENGTH

Shorter hair

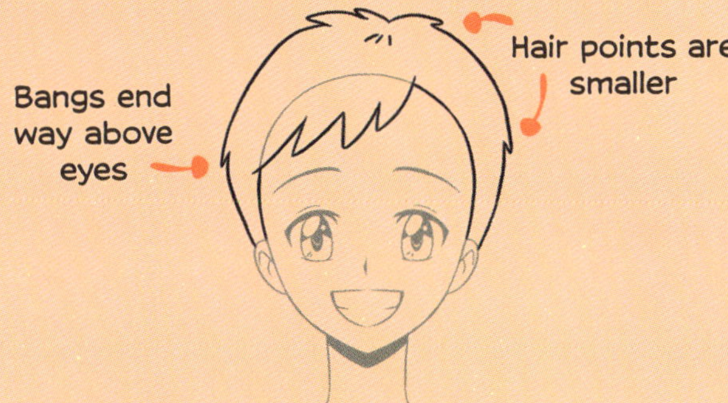

Hair has shorter, smaller points. Less of the face is covered. Try this 'do for neat, tidy characters.

Longer hair

Extended hair covers more of the face. Cool for emo, punk, or rebellious characters.

LET'S COLOR!

1 To color, start with one side of the face.

2 Next, fill in the whole face and neck.

3 Choose a hair color!

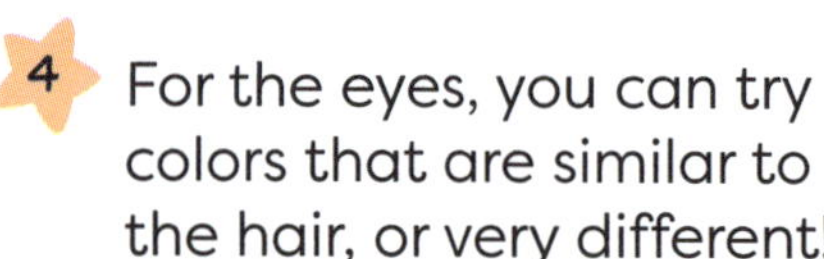

4 For the eyes, you can try colors that are similar to the hair, or very different!

NOW YOU TRY!

Make a photocopy of this head template, then practice drawing hairstyles on it! Use the lessons in Chapter 2 to help you. There are more fun hair ideas at the end of this chapter!

SIDE HAIR

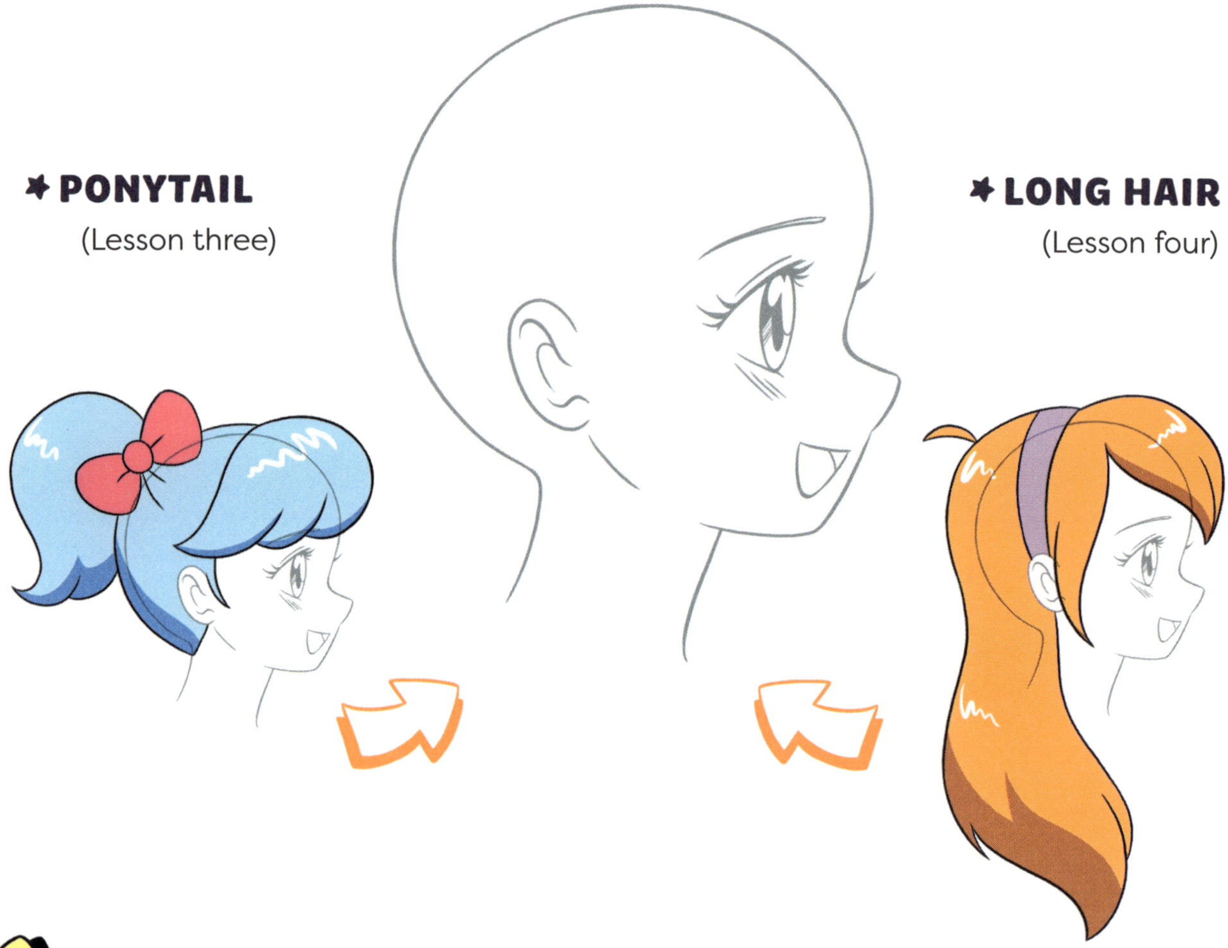

✦ PONYTAIL
(Lesson three)

✦ LONG HAIR
(Lesson four)

Let's draw these side-view hairstyles by using the head template at the end.

You'll get more hairstyle ideas at the end of this chapter, too.

First, we'll learn how to draw these two hairdos step by step. Then, use the skills you learned to create your own hairstyles on the template.

✦ LESSON THREE: PONYTAIL

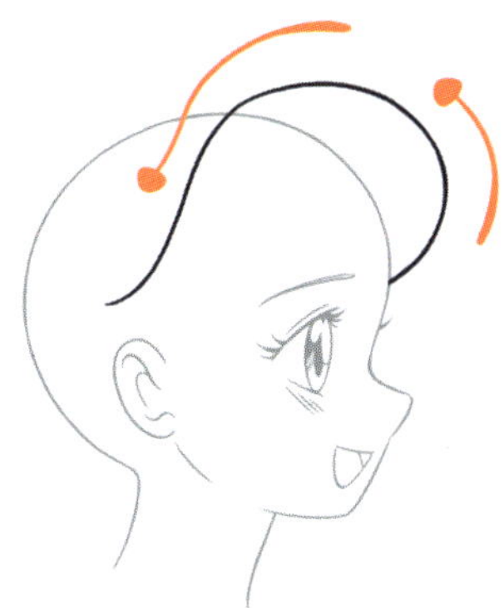

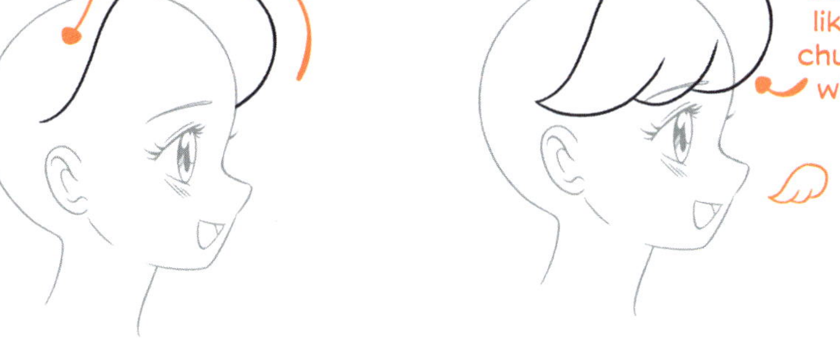

1. On the template, start the bangs with a large, curved line.
2. Finish the bangs' shape with a bumpy edge.
3. She's got a stylish bow! Draw it as a circle between two soft triangles.

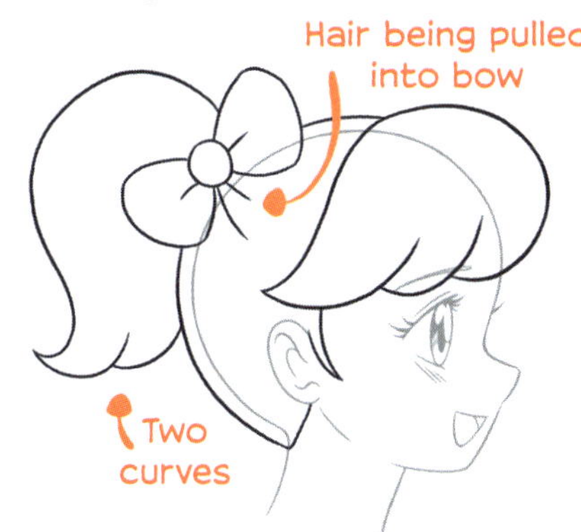

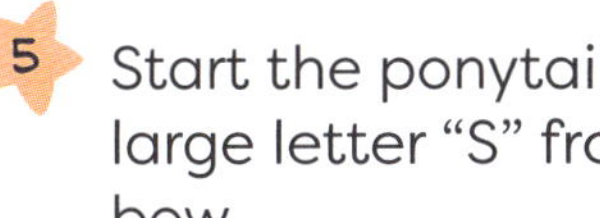

4. Draw a curved line following the round shape of the head.
5. Start the ponytail as a large letter "S" from the bow.
6. Finish the ponytail, then draw the hair line around the ear and neck.

Accessorize! Try other cute hair accessories to change your character's look.

Heart Ribbon

Cute for sweet characters.

Hair Clips

Try for book lovers or sports stars.

Crown

Great for royalty!

✦ LET'S COLOR!

1. Try another way to color: start along the edges, then go inward.
2. Fill in the face and neck with the skin color. Leave the eye area white.
3. Make her hair color stand out! I'm going with light blue.

4. Now color the rest of her hair.
5. Color the bow and eyes different colors so they stand out!

Try warm colors to make her look cozy and glowing.

Try other pretty hair and skin colors.

NOW YOU TRY!

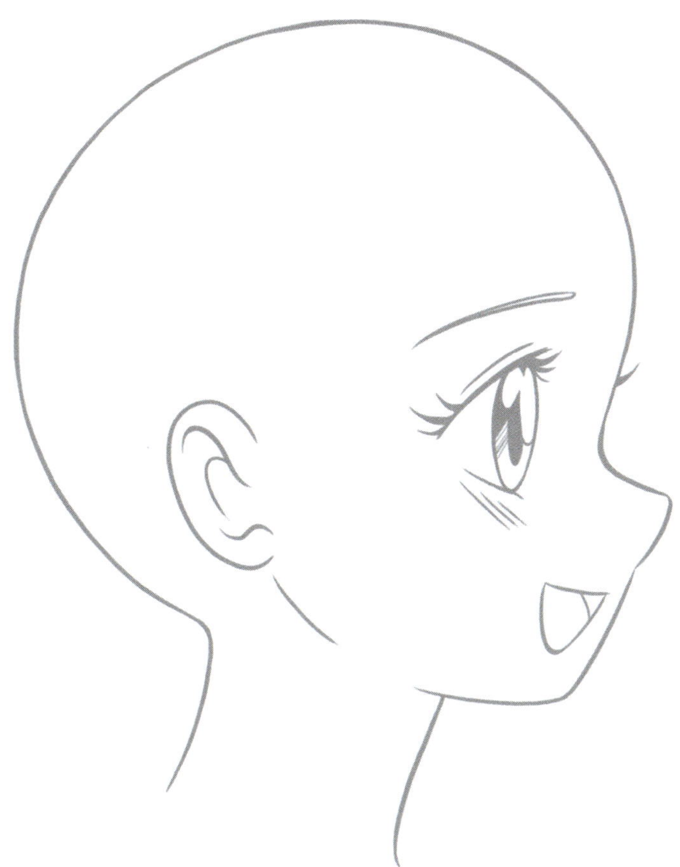

Make a photocopy of this head template, then practice drawing hairstyles on it! Use the lessons in Chapter 2 to help you. There are more fun hair ideas at the end of this chapter!

✦ LESSON FOUR: LONG HAIR

1. Draw a big curve for the bangs above the template's forehead.

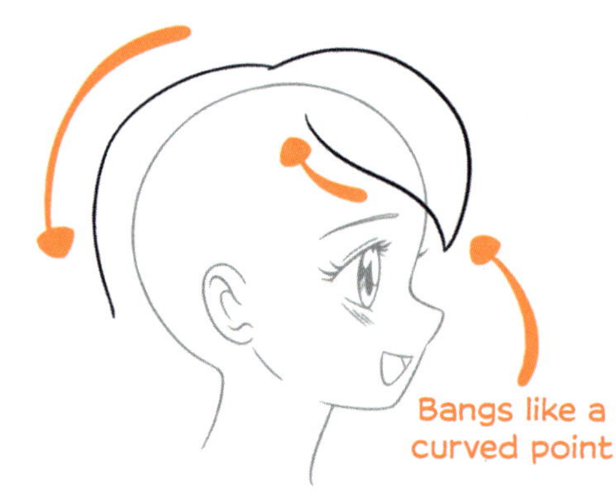

2. Draw another curve for the bangs' other edge. Then add the back of the hair as a larger curve.

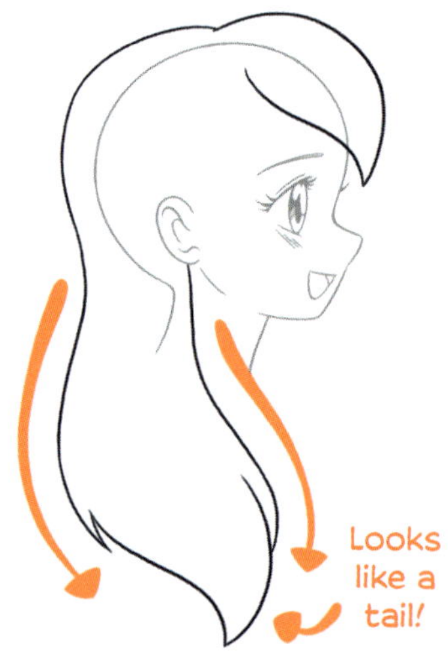

3. Now draw the long hair coming down as flowy lines that end in a thick point.

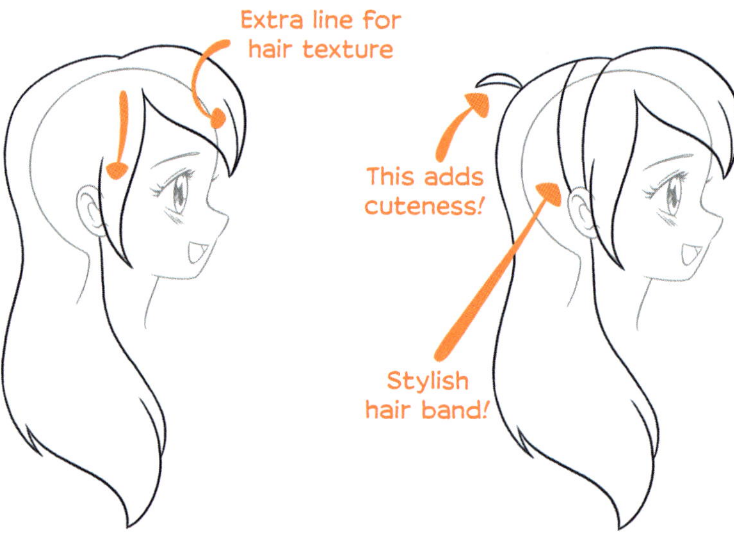

4. Complete the hair around the face with a slim, triangular piece going down past the ear.

5. Let's add some finishing touches, like a cute piece of hair poking up at the back, and a stylish hair band.

Change the look of your character by varying the hair length!

Long hair:
Flowing and elegant! Try for princesses, royalty, popular girls, or magical characters.

Medium-length hair:
Can end around the neck or shoulders.

Short hair:
Cute and stylish! Can be nice for girly, sporty, or tomboyish characters.

Which one will you choose?

TYPES OF HAIR ENDS

You can make your character look different just by changing how the hair ends at their tips:

Flat hair tip:
Hair with flat edges can create a rigid or sturdy look—like it has lots of hair gel.

Pointed hair tip:
Natural hair tips can make a hairdo look realistic.

Rounded hair tip:
Rounded hair tips can make a character look cuter, softer, or friendlier!

There are so many ways to design hair! The possibilities are endless!

LET'S COLOR!

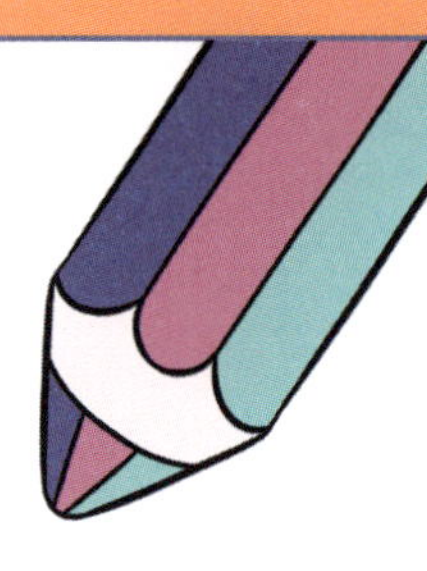

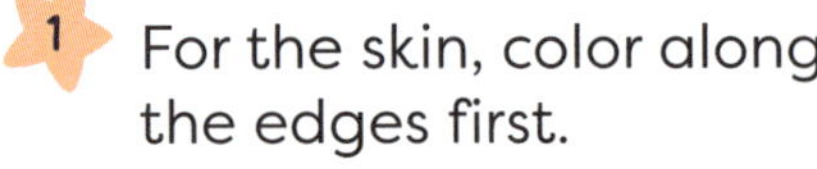

1 For the skin, color along the edges first.

2 Now fill in the face and neck. Leave the eye area white.

3 Pick a hair color you like! Start with the front part.

4 Color the rest of the hair, leaving the hair band white.

5 Now color the hair band, eye, and mouth. Use white gel pens for hair highlights, and brown for some hair shadow.

Make her into an ice princess or magical character with white-blue hair and light purple skin.

Try darker hair colors with light hair bands for striking contrast!

NOW YOU TRY!

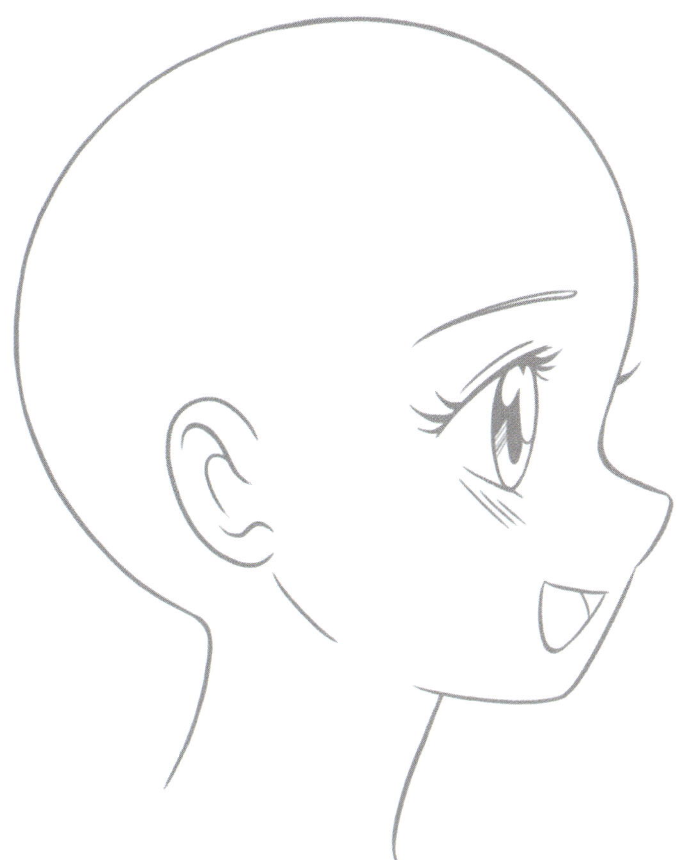

Make a photocopy of this head template, then practice drawing hairstyles on it! Use the lessons in Chapter 2 to help you. There are more fun hair ideas at the end of this chapter!

BONUS IDEAS

Hairy good! You're done with Chapter 2! Try these fun hairdos on the templates!

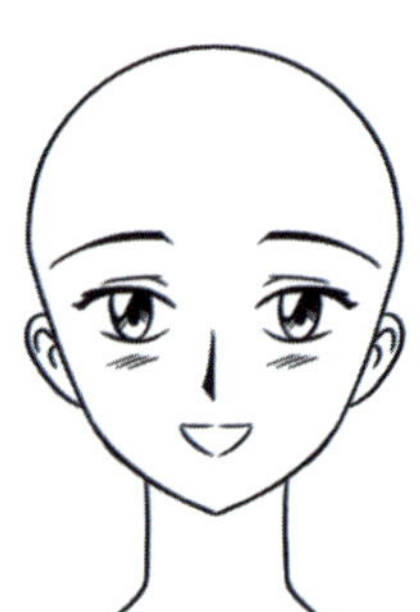

Cool and stylish!

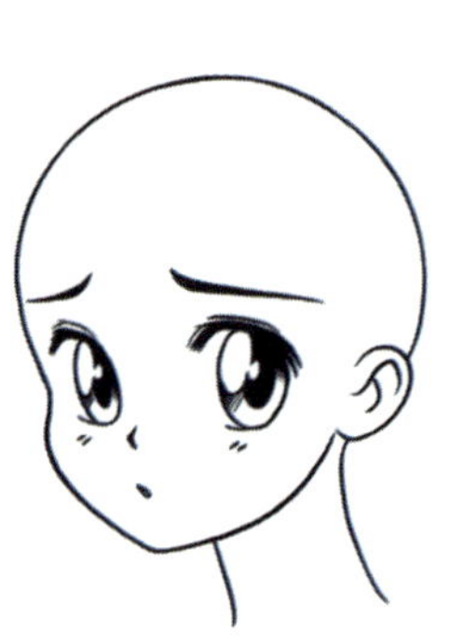

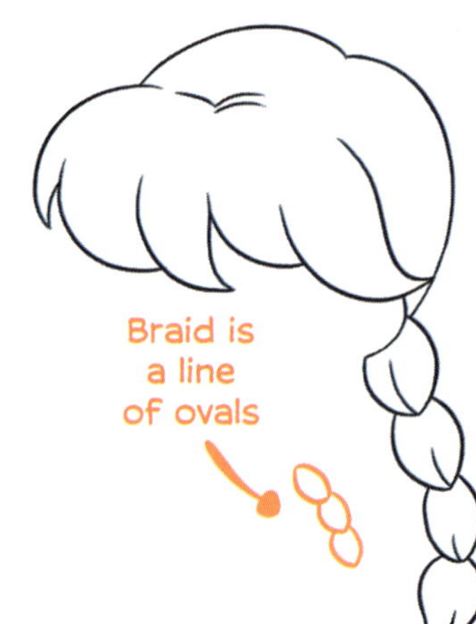

She's not sure how her school photo turned out . . .

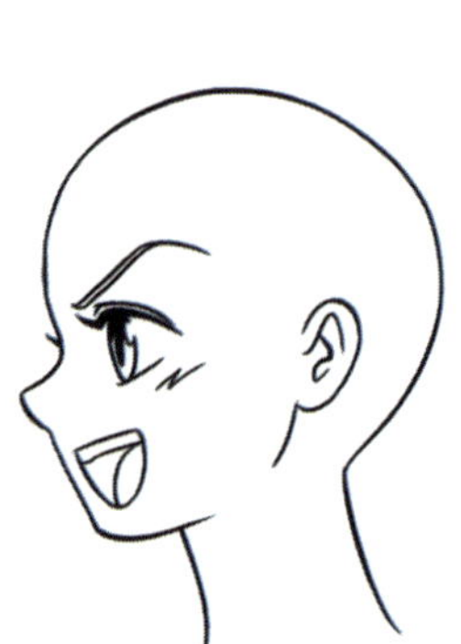

With hair this bright, you can see her from miles away!

Two hair buns: double the cuteness!

Hair lines are round and soft!

Did she just see a cute puppy?

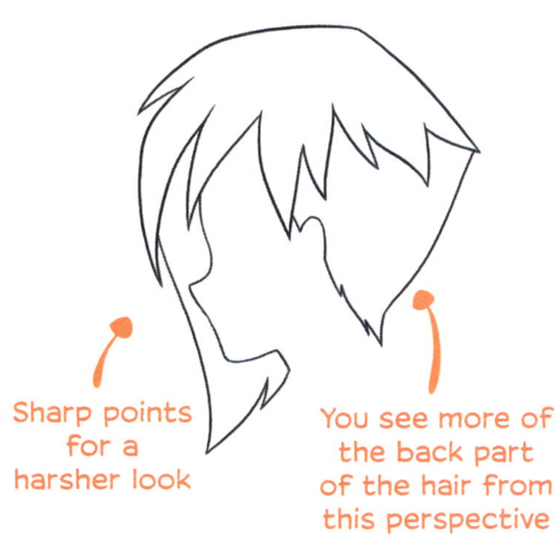

Sharp points for a harsher look

You see more of the back part of the hair from this perspective

His friend just ate his pizza slice!

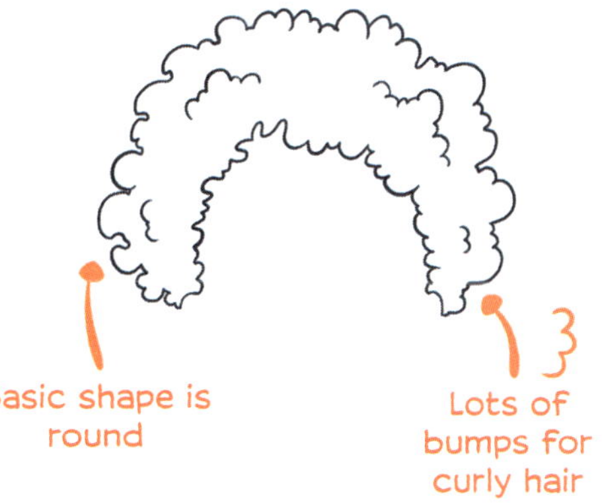

Basic shape is round

Lots of bumps for curly hair

He likes his freckles!

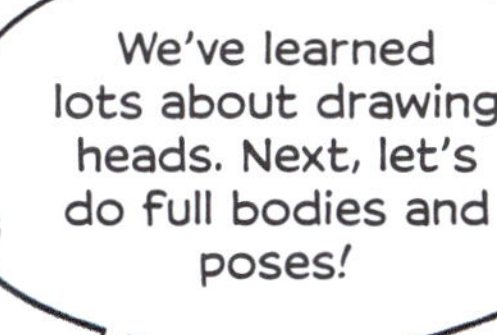

We've learned lots about drawing heads. Next, let's do full bodies and poses!

EXTRA TEMPLATES

Here are extra head templates from Chapter 2 for you to practice drawing hairstyles!

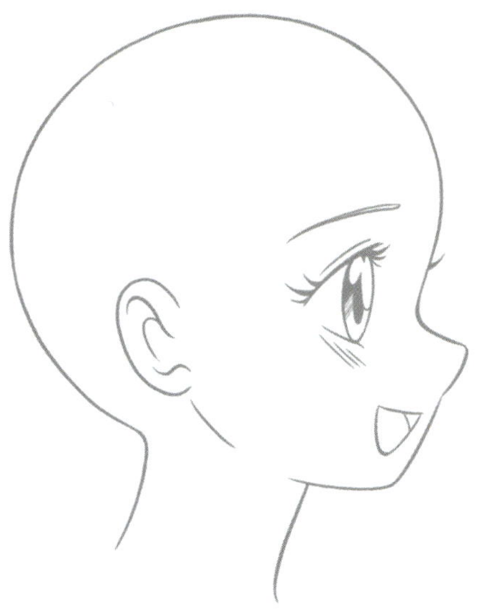

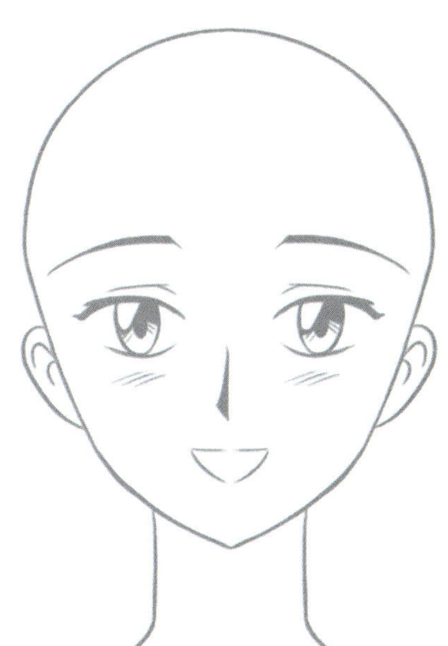

Let's design simplified characters from head to toe in fun poses!

3

BODIES AND BASIC POSES

LESSON ONE: STANDING POSE

In this chapter, we'll learn how to draw a pose using the basic body as our template!

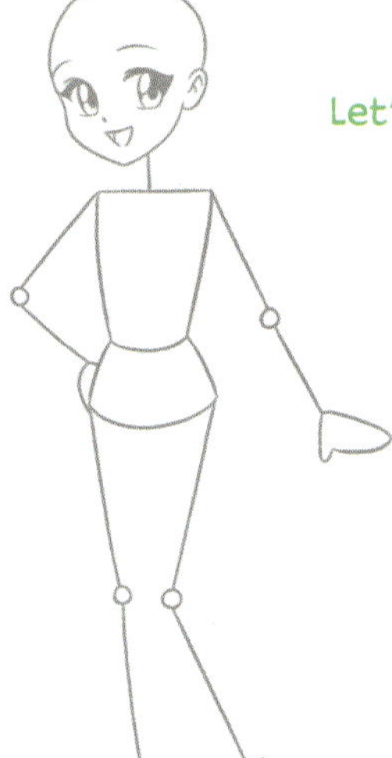

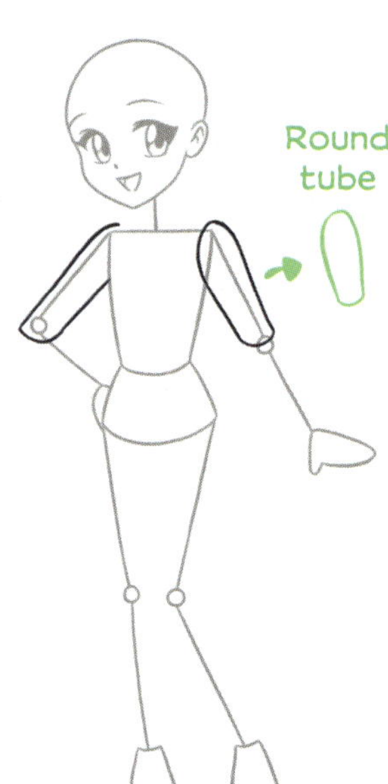

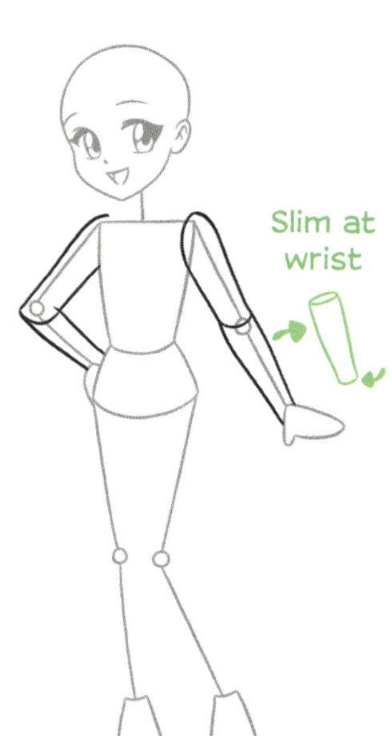

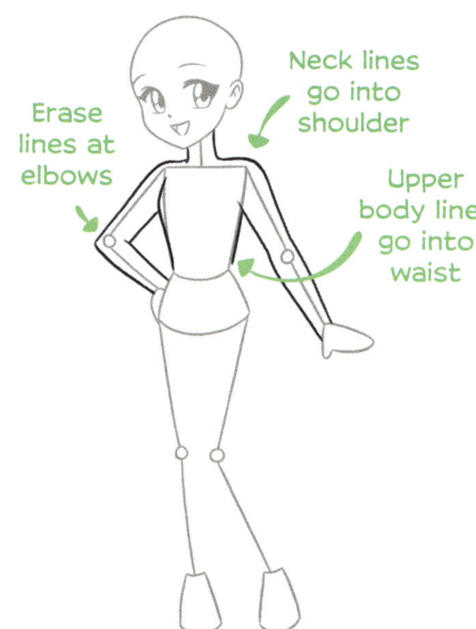

1. Start with upper arms like round tubes that end at the elbows.
2. Draw thinner tubes for the lower arms.
3. Draw a neck. Use the template's body to draw the chest and waist.

Note: We're focusing on bodies and poses, so the outfits in this chapter will be basic. Learn different outfits in the next chapter.

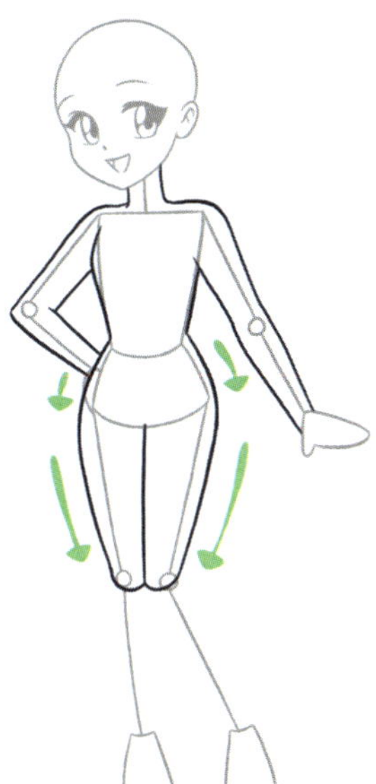

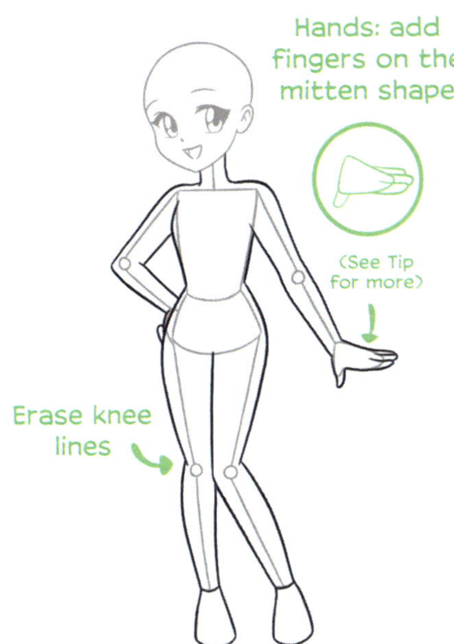

4 Follow the template—draw hips curving out. Make the upper legs big tubes ending at the knees.

5 Draw the lower legs like thin tubes that narrow at the ankles.

6 Use the template's wedge feet to draw feet lines. For hands, add fingers to the mitten shape.

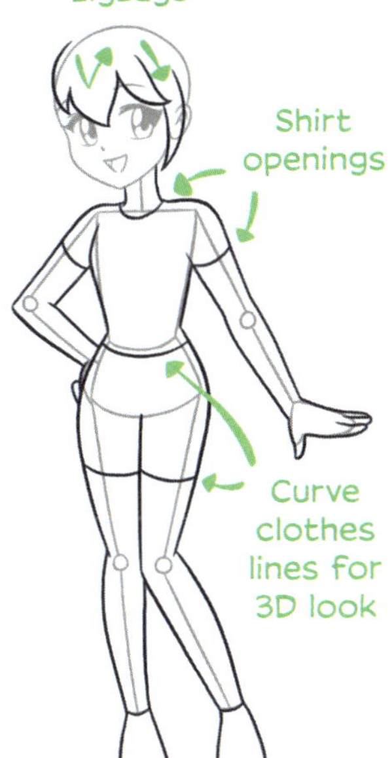

7 Now draw clothes with curved edges on the limbs, waist, and neck. Start the hair!

8 Complete the hair, trace the face so the lines stand out, and we're ready to color!

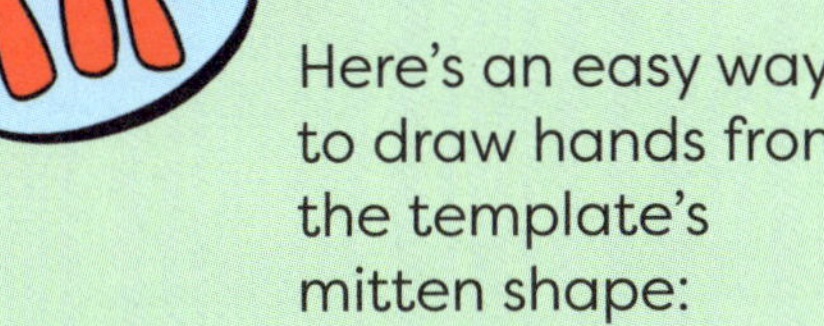

Here's an easy way to draw hands from the template's mitten shape:

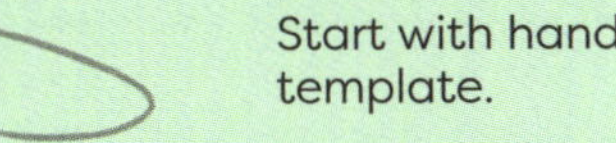

Start with hand template.

Add a finger as a bump coming out. Add thumb.

Repeat finger bumps two more times. (You can't see all the fingers in this view.)

LET'S COLOR!

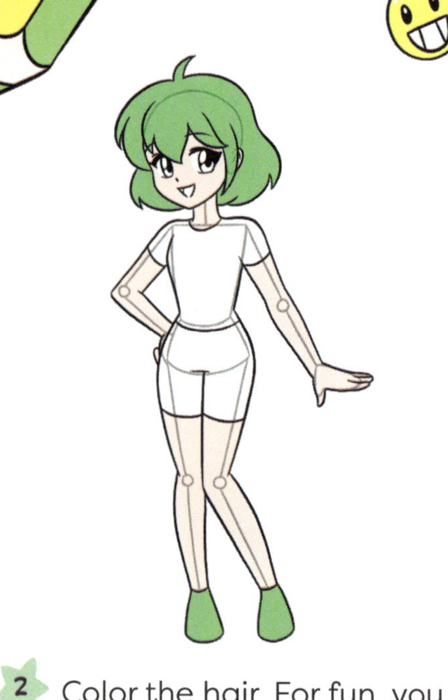

1 Start with the skin color. Choose any you like!

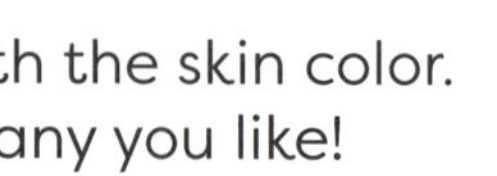

2 Color the hair. For fun, you can have the shoes match!

3 Choose bright colors for the clothes. Then color the eyes and mouth.

4 This step is optional. If you want a more 3D look, use darker colors to shade the hair, shoes, and neck.

OTHER COLORS

Try other colors or add designs on the clothing to make your character uniquely your own!

Natural hair colors can make your character look down to earth. The striped shorts can make her look sporty!

Color the sleeves and shirt differently for bold designs! Try logos on the shirt, which will make her look more casual or punk.

NOW YOU TRY!

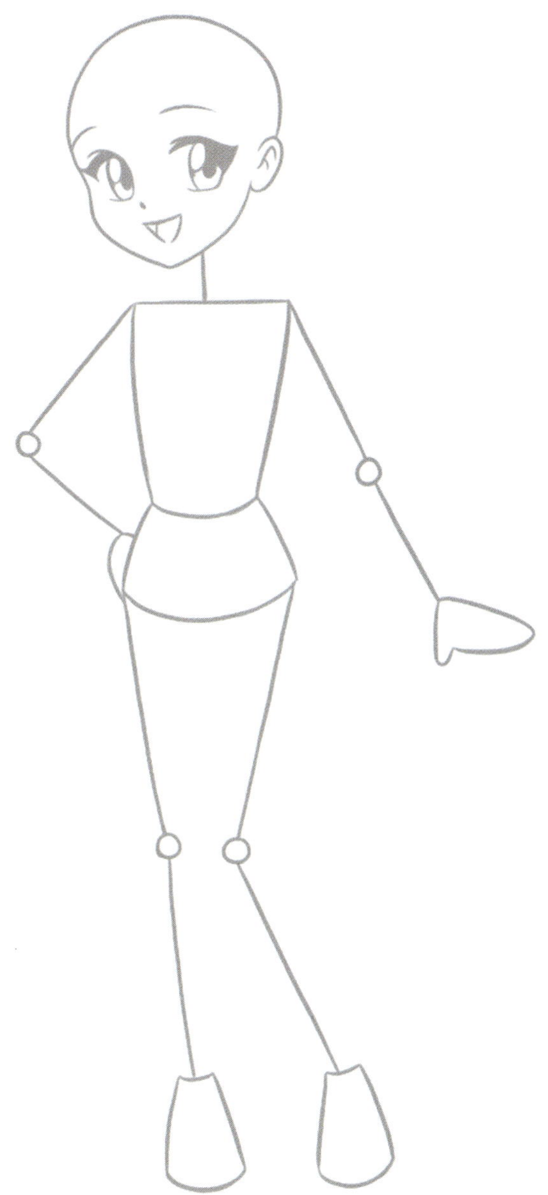

Make a photocopy of this body template, then practice drawing the pose on it! Use the lessons in Chapter 3 to help you. There are more fun pose ideas at the end of this chapter!

✦ LESSON TWO: SITTING POSE

Try this pose for kids sitting in class, at home, or at the beach, or hanging out with friends!

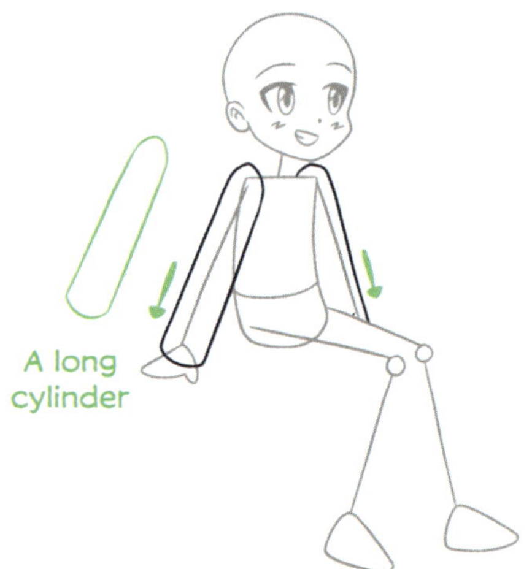

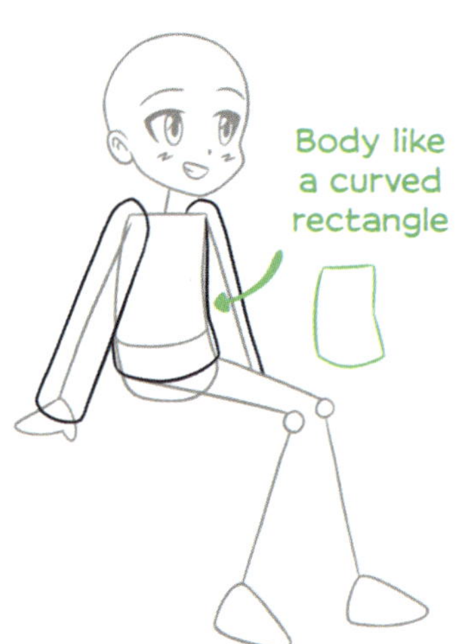

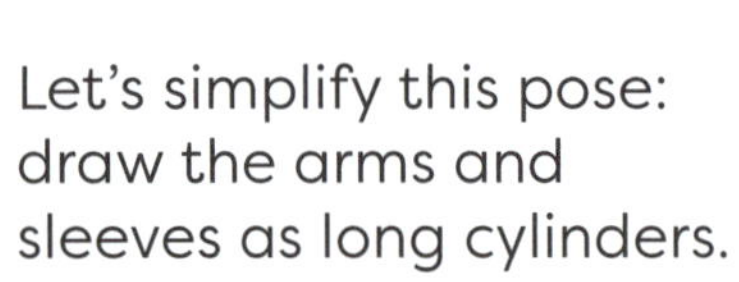

1. Let's simplify this pose: draw the arms and sleeves as long cylinders.

2. Follow the template's body: add a curved rectangle. This will be part of his hoodie, too.

3. Under the hoodie, draw the upper legs coming out like round cylinders.

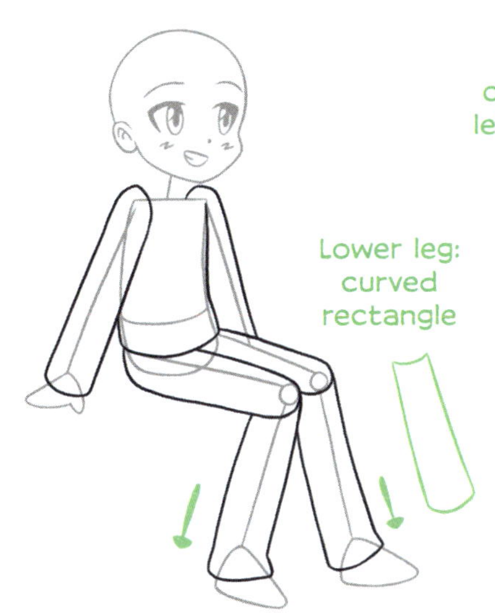

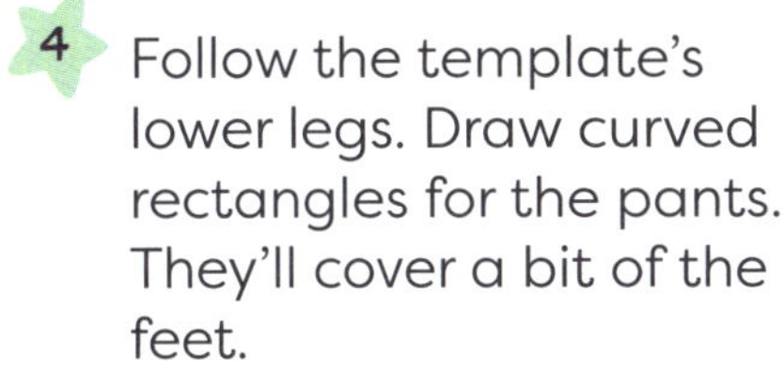

4 Follow the template's lower legs. Draw curved rectangles for the pants. They'll cover a bit of the feet.

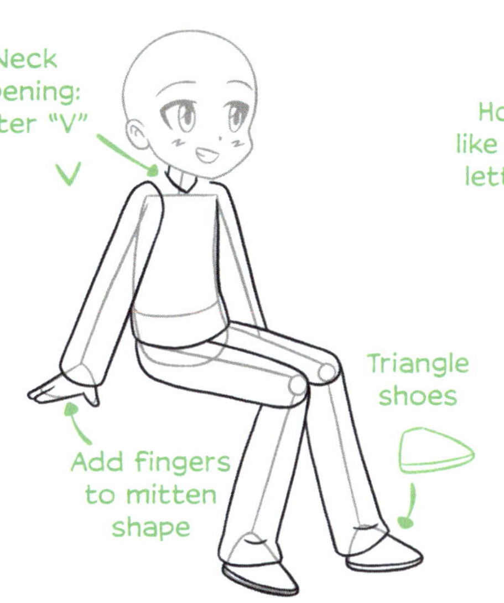

5 Add fingers to the hands, then draw the shoes on the triangle feet shapes.

6 Draw a "V" for a hood, then start the hair!

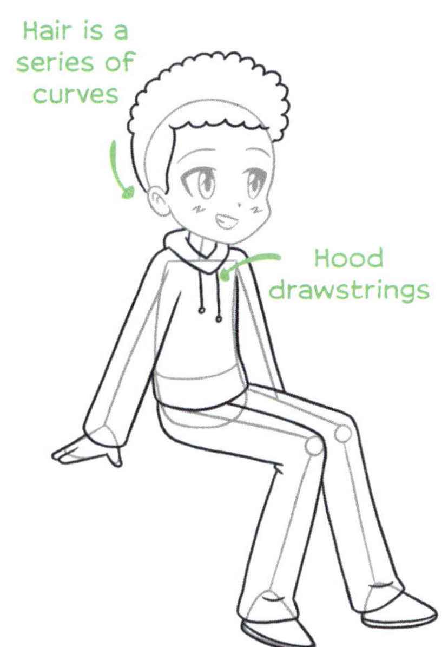

7 Finish drawing the curly hair with lots of curves. Add drawstrings to the hood.

8 Trace over the face lines so they stand out!

Try other bottoms to change his look:

Shorts: energetic and sporty

Baggy pants: cool and casual

Which will you choose?

LET'S COLOR!

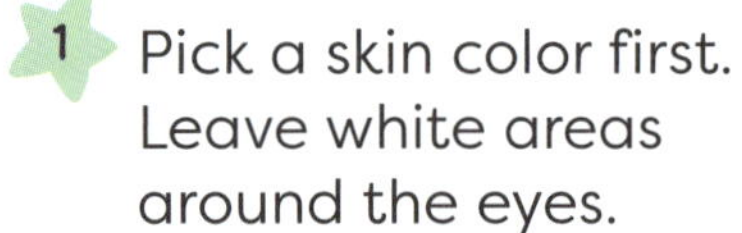

1 Pick a skin color first. Leave white areas around the eyes.

2 Color parts of the hoodie and hair. I'm using reds for a warm look.

3 Now use a contrasting color for the pants so they stand out.

4 Color the eyes, shoes, and ledge. Use a white gel pen for the sleeve stripes to make him look sporty.

Pick a bright color and black for a striking feel! He looks energetic.

Use all cool colors for the hair and clothes for a calm and chill look.

Which will you choose?

NOW YOU TRY!

Make a photocopy of this body template, then practice drawing the pose on it! Use the lessons in Chapter 3 to help you. There are more fun pose ideas at the end of this chapter!

★ LESSON THREE: FLYING POSE

This pose is great for angels, magical girls, and superheroes. Or it can be for kids jumping on their beds!

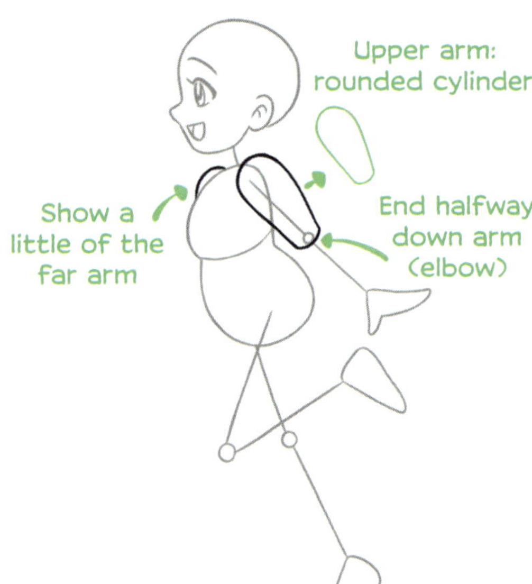

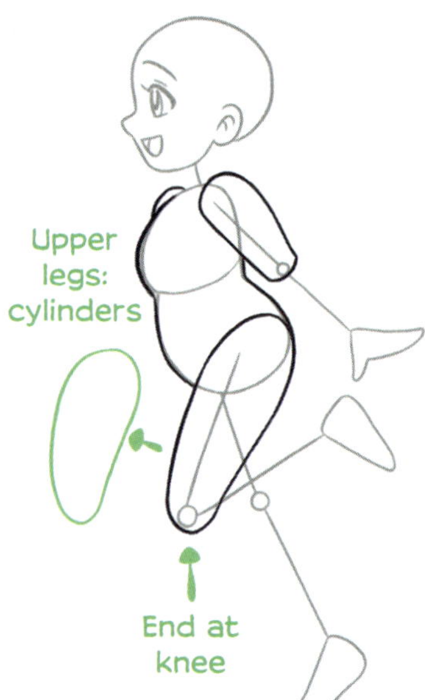

1. Start with cylinders for the upper arms. The far arm is mostly hidden.
2. Follow the template's body and draw slightly curved lines for the front and back.
3. Now add a large, stretched oval for the upper leg.

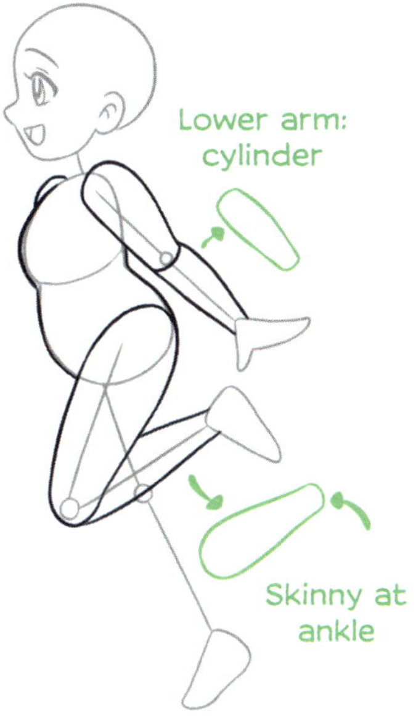

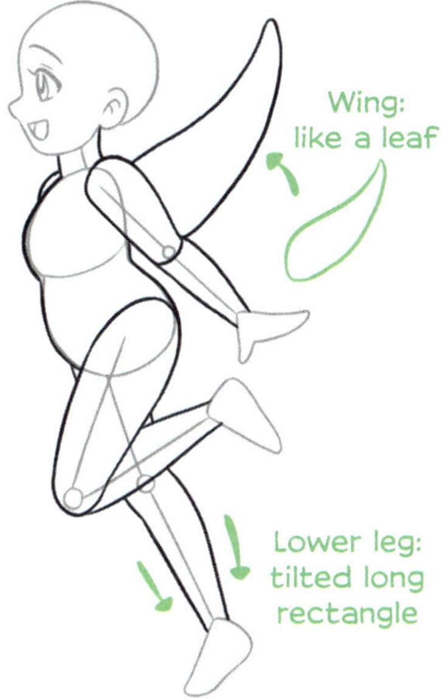

4 Draw the lower arm as a rounded cylinder. The lower leg is like a long rectangle that gets skinny at the ankle.

5 Add a magical touch with a wing! It's like a leaf shape first. Then draw the far leg.

6 Make the wing shape into feathers with bumps along the edge. Draw fingers, feet, and clothes lines at the neck and waist.

7 Draw long, flowing hair with soft curves!

8 Trace over the template's face lines with a dark pen so they stand out!

TIP

Try other types of wings to make your character look very different!

Bat wings:
edgy or spooky

Fairy wings:
natural and pretty

Which will you choose?

LET'S COLOR!

1 Let's start by coloring her skin. Leave white areas around the eyes.

2 Now color her hair. I'm using bright yellow for a sunny, friendly look.

3 Try cool colors for the outfit to contrast with the warm hair.

4 To add dimension, use orange to shade the hair, and darker colors to shade the neck and the far leg.

OTHER COLORS

Which will you choose?

Try a darker skin tone with bright colors! It's fun to match the hair color with the shoes.

Use wild colors for a completely fantastical look! Don't be afraid to try different combinations!

NOW YOU TRY!

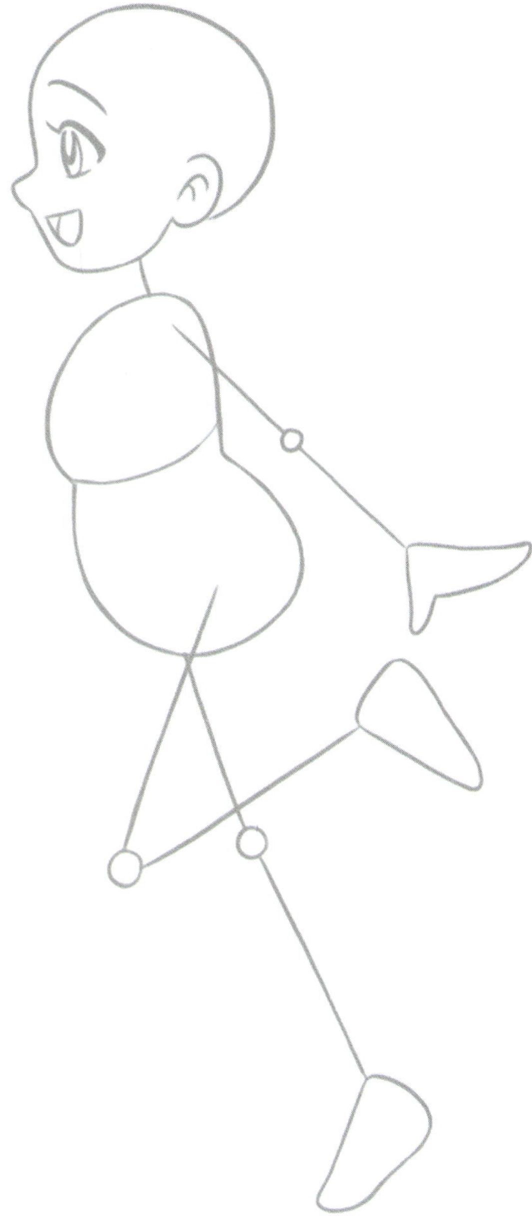

Make a photocopy of this body template, then practice drawing the pose on it! Use the lessons in Chapter 3 to help you. There are more fun pose ideas at the end of this chapter!

✦ LESSON FOUR: ACTION POSE

Watch out! This pose is great for action heroes, villains, sports stars, or adventurers!

Let's go from a body template to an action pose.

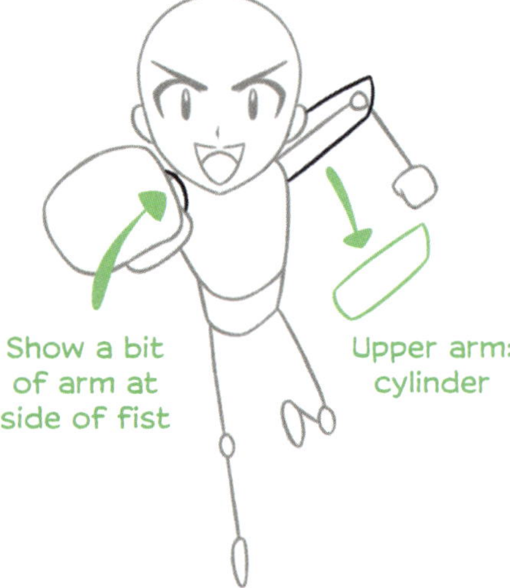

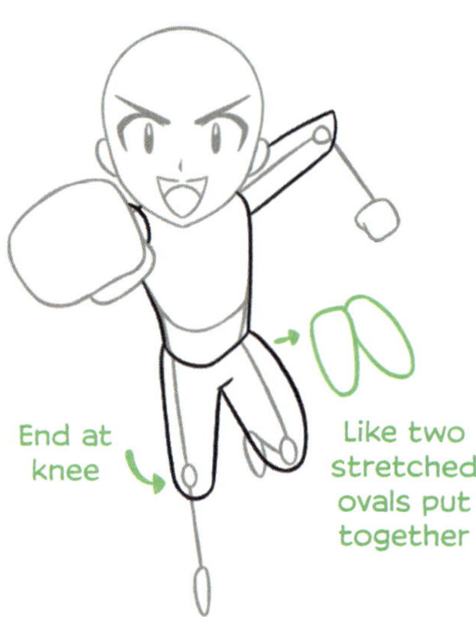

1. Start with cylinders for the upper arms. The fist will cover almost all of the closer arm.

2. Follow the template's body and draw lines for the torso (the chest and waist).

3. The upper legs are stretched ovals. The bent leg will cover most of that foot.

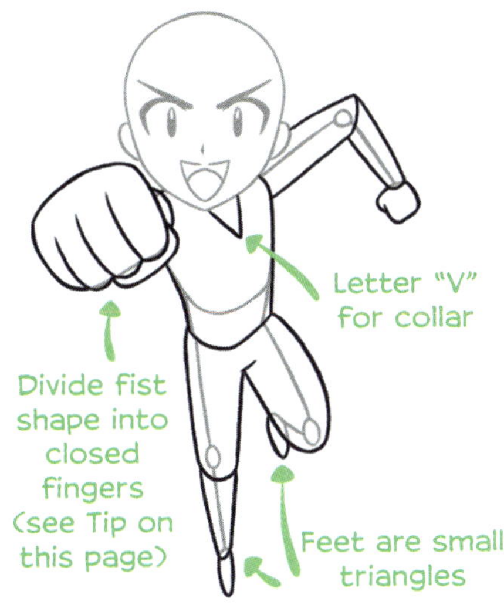

4 Add cylinders for the lower arm and leg. You can't see the lower part of the bent leg.

5 Draw the outlines of the hands and feet. For the fist, divide it into fingers with three lines.

6 Now that the body's done, let's make a cool hairdo! Start with a jagged shape for the bangs.

Big because it's closer to you

Tiny because it's farther away

7 Complete the rest of the hair as curved zigzags.

8 Trace over the template's face lines with a dark pen so they stand out!

Tip

Here's a closer look at how to draw an easy fist using the template:

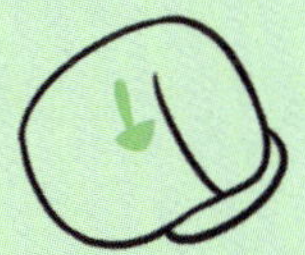

LET'S COLOR!

1 Color the skin, with white areas left around the eyes.

2 Add colors for the hair and shirt. I'm leaving the sleeves to do as a different color in the next step.

3 Color the sleeves, pants, and feet.

4 Add some darker blues into the hair for shadows so it looks more dimensional. Color the mouth, too!

Which will you choose?

Try alien colors for a sci-fi look! Draw designs on his clothing so it looks like a space suit or superhero outfit.

Contrast light hair with darker skin for a striking look. Add little blue shadows to make the light hair complete.

NOW YOU TRY!

Make a photocopy of this body template, then practice drawing the pose on it! Use the lessons in Chapter 3 to help you. There are more fun pose ideas at the end of this chapter!

BONUS IDEAS

Now you're done with Chapter 3! Design more fun poses with these body templates!

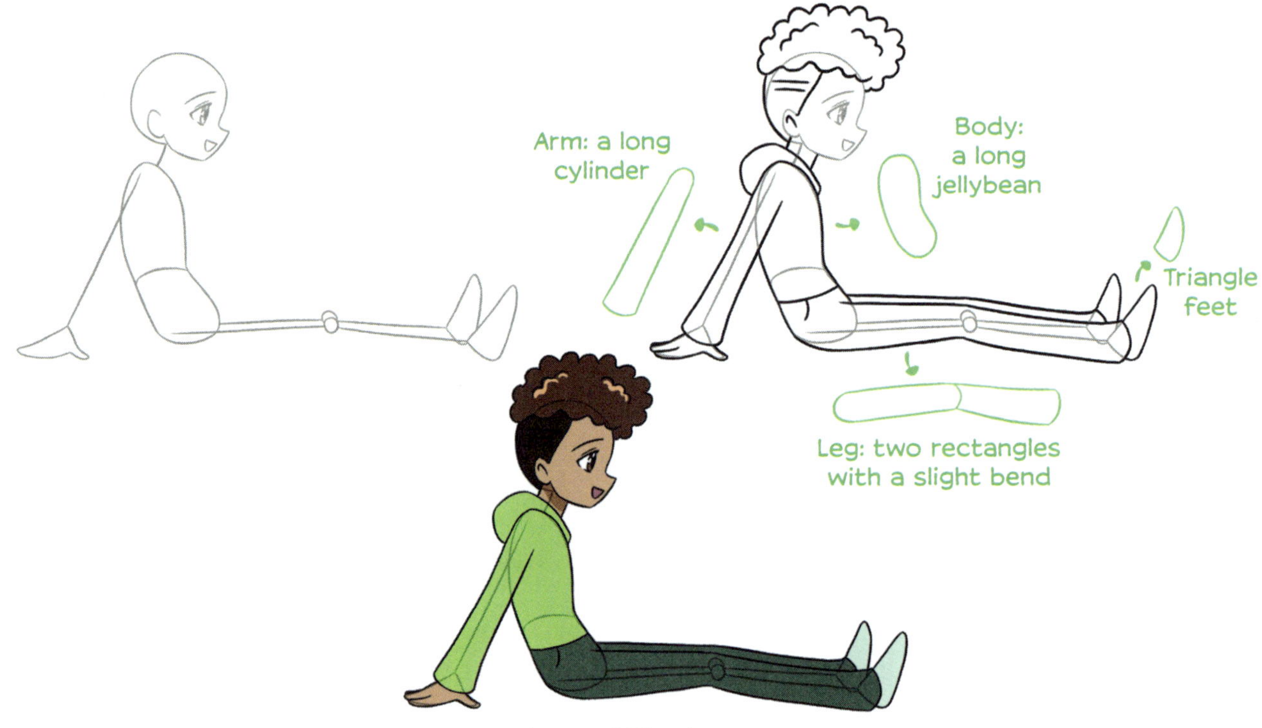

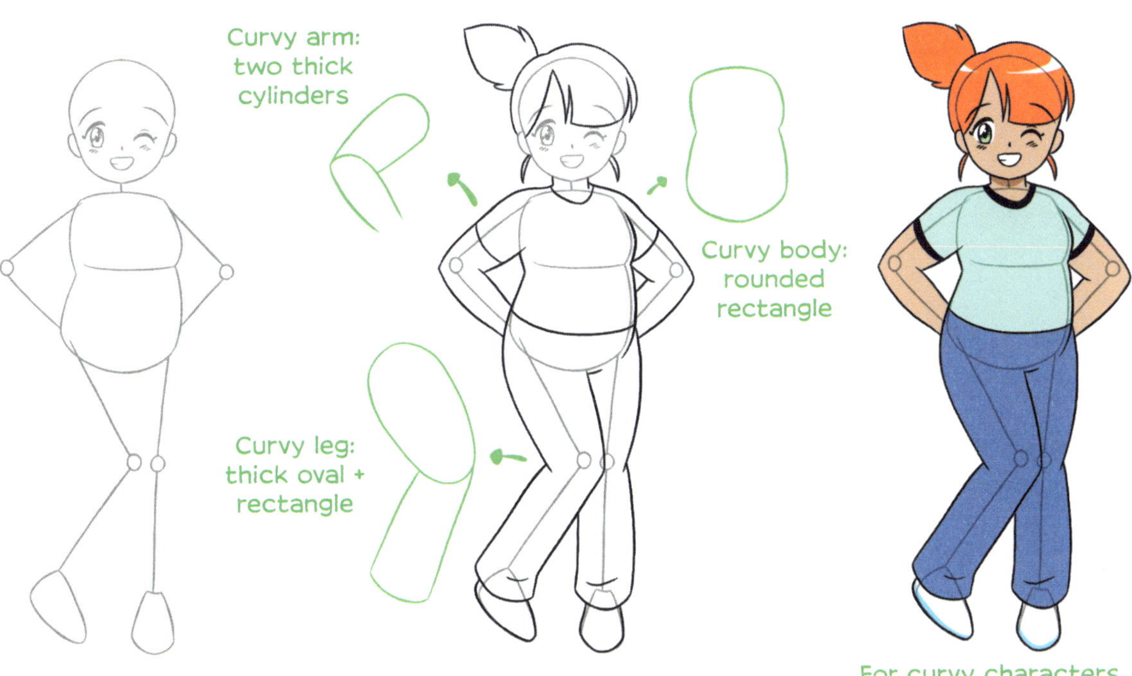

For curvy characters, make the body shapes wider

Since we've learned about drawing bodies, let's design cool outfits in the next chapter!

EXTRA TEMPLATES

You can photocopy these to practice as much as you want!

Here are extra body templates from Chapter 3 for you to practice drawing poses!

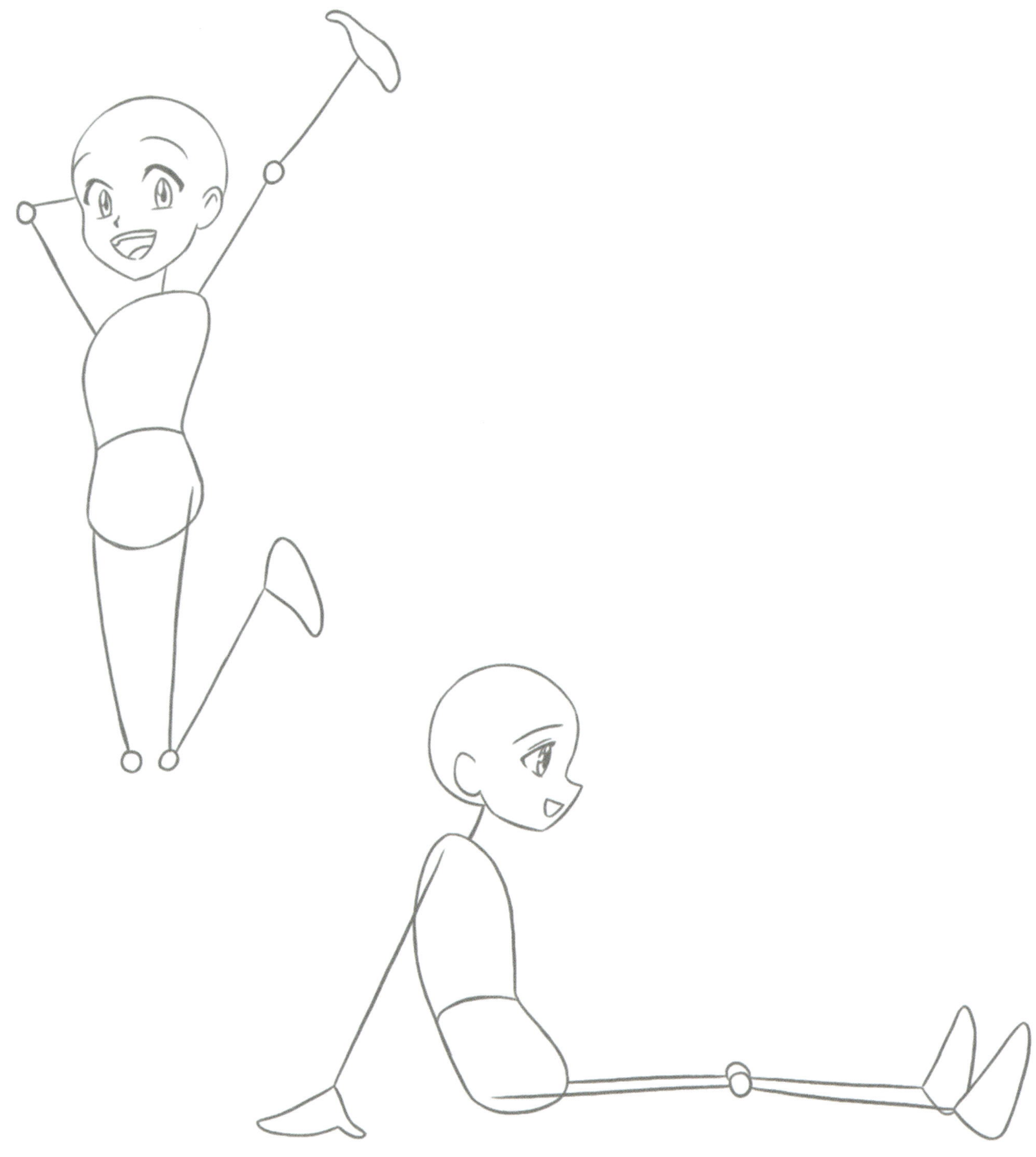

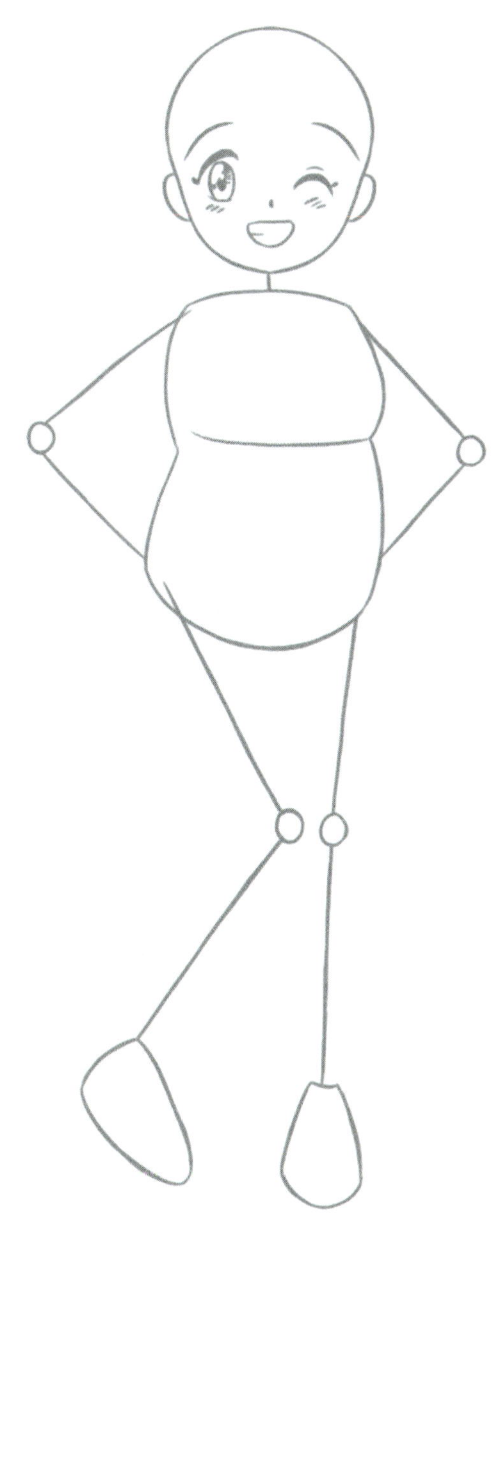

Unleash your inner fashion designer and draw cool, fun outfits for all kinds of characters!

4

OUTFITS

LESSON ONE: COOL SUPERHERO SUIT

Let's learn how to draw outfits on top of the complete body templates!

Let's go from a body template to a finished superhero in his suit!

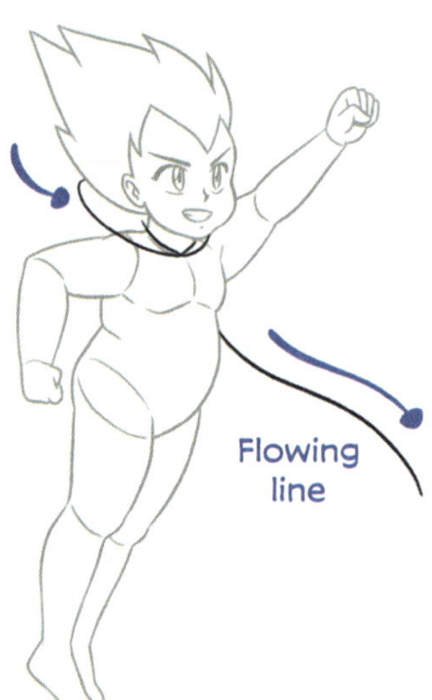

Letter "V" as suit design

Cape folds here

1. Begin the cape with a large, flowing line going down. Draw the wide collar around the neck.
2. Draw the other side of the cape behind the body.
3. Add a fold in the cape at the bottom corner and a "V" to the suit design.

Note: Since we have learned about drawing bodies and poses, these body templates have the finished pose already. We will focus just on drawing clothes for this chapter!

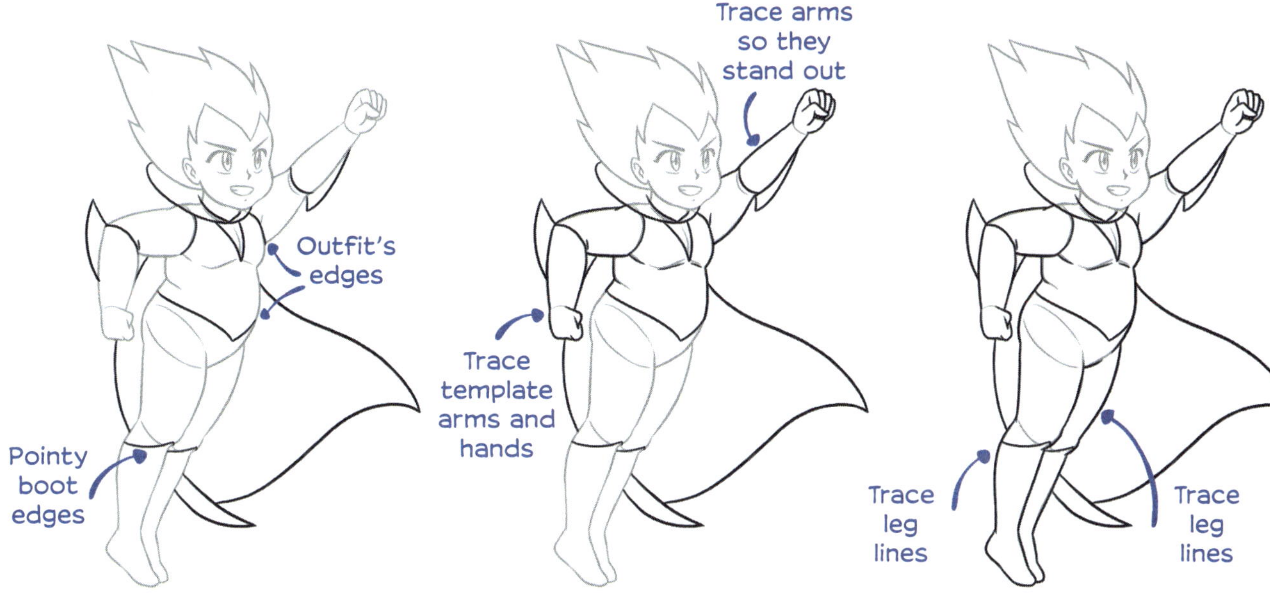

4 Draw more edges and lines for the suit and boots. Add cool, pointy pieces sticking out of the arms of the suit!

5 Trace over the arm and hand lines of the template so they stand out.

6 Now go over the template's leg and feet lines so they show better.

7 Lastly, trace over the head and face lines on the template. Start the hair!

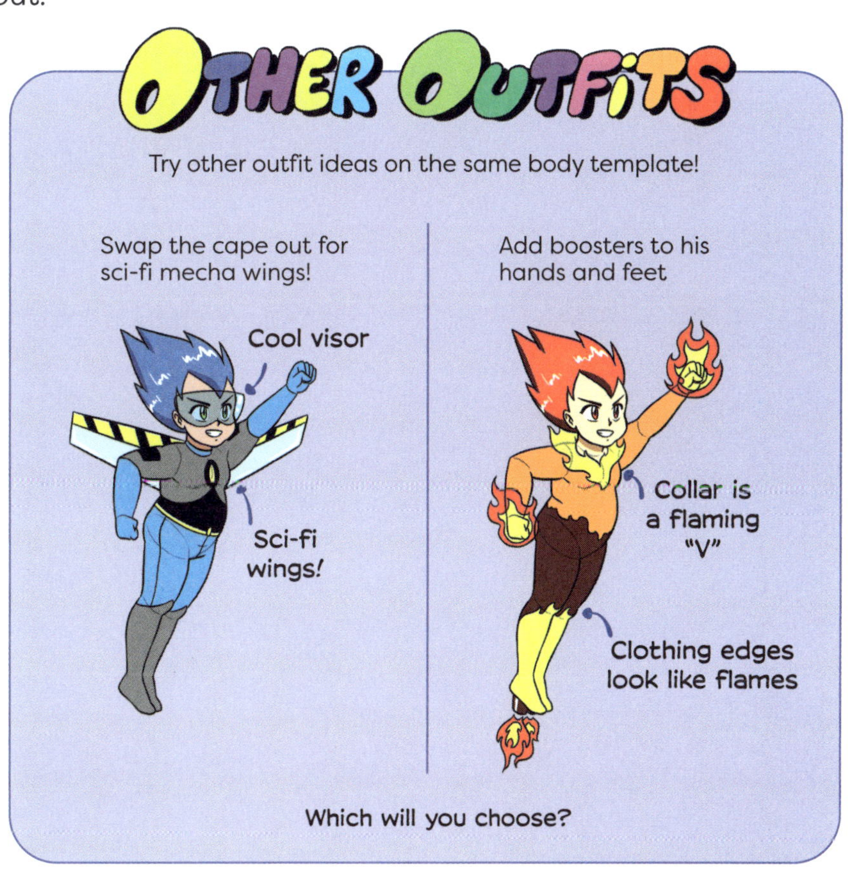

✦ LET'S COLOR!

1. Start with the skin color. Choose any you like! Leave the areas around the eyes white.

2. Color the hair. Go for wild, bright, or natural. For fun, I'm matching the hair with parts of the outfit.

3. Choose bright and dark colors for the rest of the outfit. Color the eyes.

4. For a more 3D look, use a white gel pen for the shiny hair highlights. Add dark colors to shade the cape.

NOW YOU TRY!

Make a photocopy of this body template, then practice drawing the clothes on it! Use the lessons in Chapter 4 to help you. There are more fun outfit ideas at the end of this chapter!

✦ LESSON TWO: CAT HOODIE & SHORTS

This is a fun outfit for cute or silly characters! Change the hoodie's ears to a different animal's if you like.

Let's go from a body template to a fun girl in a cat hoodie and shorts!

△

Cat ears: triangles

Opening part of hood surrounds face

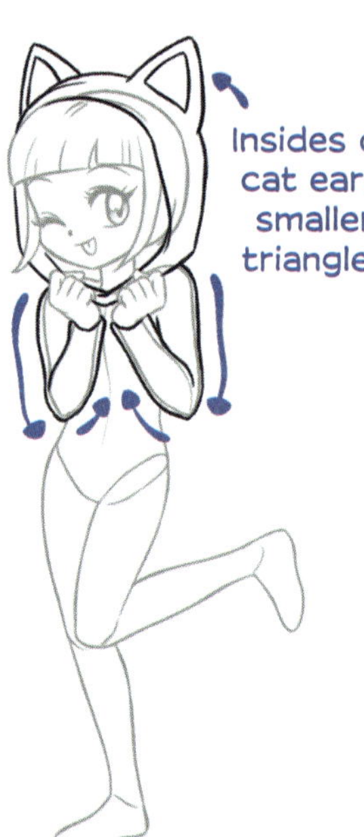

1. Start the hood part with a large, round shape around the head, ending below the neck.

2. Add the cute cat ears on the hood! Also draw the opening of the hood as curves around the face.

3. Follow the template's arms to draw the sleeves. Then, add the inner areas to the cat ears.

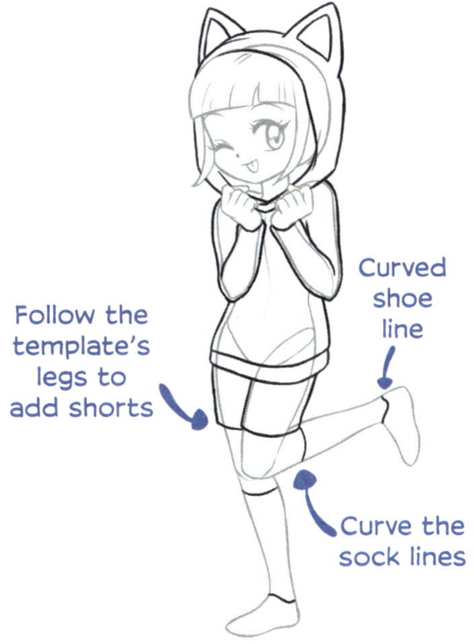

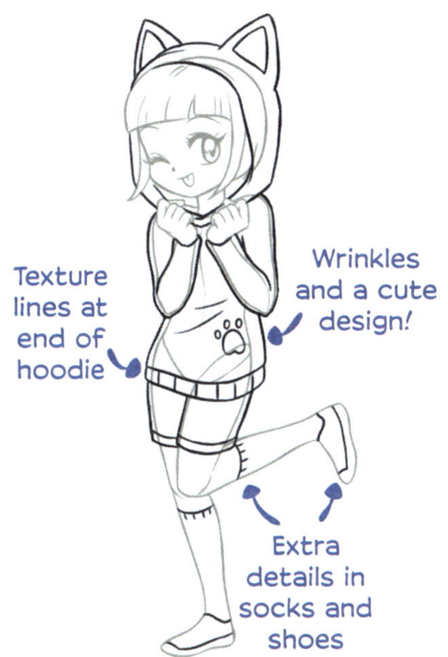

4 Follow the template's body to draw the rest of the hoodie down to the hips.

5 Add shorts that end above the knees. Then draw curves for the socks and shoes.

6 Finish the details of the clothing with texture lines and designs.

7 Now trace the template's head and leg lines so they stand out!

✦ LET'S COLOR!

1. Color the skin first. Leave a white area around the eye.

2. Now choose a fun color for the cat hoodie! Try something bright to make it stand out.

3. For the hair, try a very different color from the hoodie. Then color the eye, shorts, and shoes.

4. This step is optional. To add dimension, use a light gel pen to draw the hair's highlight. Use darker blue, green, and brown to shade the skin and clothing.

Which will you choose?

For a bright, sunny look, try yellows! She looks energetic.

Try red to grab attention!

NOW YOU TRY!

Make a photocopy of this body template, then practice drawing the clothes on it! Use the lessons in Chapter 4 to help you. There are more fun outfit ideas at the end of this chapter!

LESSON THREE: PRETTY DRESS

Design a pretty dress for characters who are models, pretty people, glam stars on the red carpet, or fashionistas!

Let's go from a body template to a beautiful model in a pretty dress!

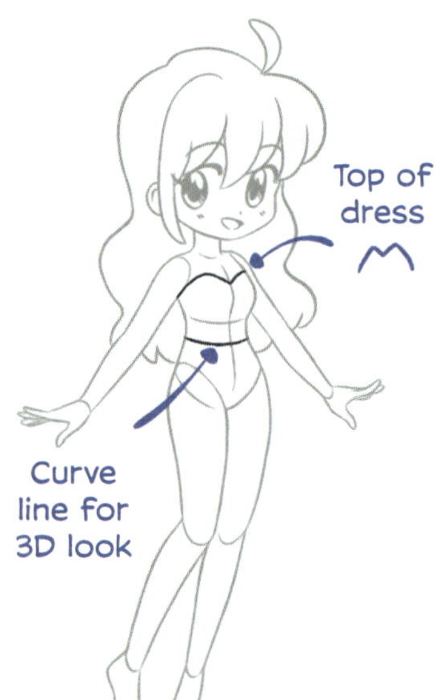

1 Begin her dress with a top that fits snug around the chest.

2 Fan out the bottom for the wide dress.

3 For a pretty look, draw the bottom edge of the dress with waves.

4 Draw cute shoulder straps at the top part of the dress. In the middle, add a cute heart and waistline. Draw a hair bow and stylish shoes.

5 Add more details to the dress like another waistline to make a belt. Draw cute bows on the shoes.

6 Trace the lines of the template's arms and legs.

7 Now trace the face and hair lines on the template so they stand out!

LET'S COLOR!

1. Begin with coloring her skin. Leave white areas around the eyes.

2. Use a fun color for her hair! I chose pink for a cute look. Match the belt and shoes with the hair.

3. Use very different colors for the dress, bows, and eyes so they stand out.

4. To add dimension, use dark pink to shade the hair. With a white gel pen, draw squiggly highlights on the hair! Use darker peach and darker blue to shade the skin and dress.

Which will you choose?

Make the dress and shoes match with lively colors!

Try blues and yellows so she stands out!

NOW YOU TRY!

Make a photocopy of this body template, then practice drawing the clothes on it! Use the lessons in Chapter 4 to help you. There are more fun outfit ideas at the end of this chapter!

★ LESSON FOUR: COOL WARRIOR COSTUME

This armored costume is great for fantasy warriors, wizards, or magical characters!

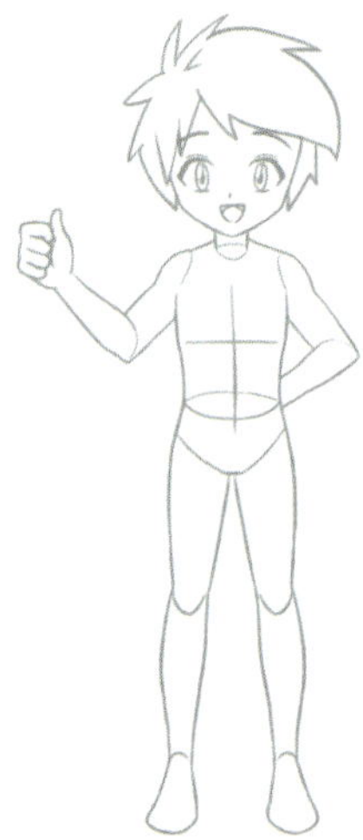

Let's go from a body template to a warrior in his cool costume!

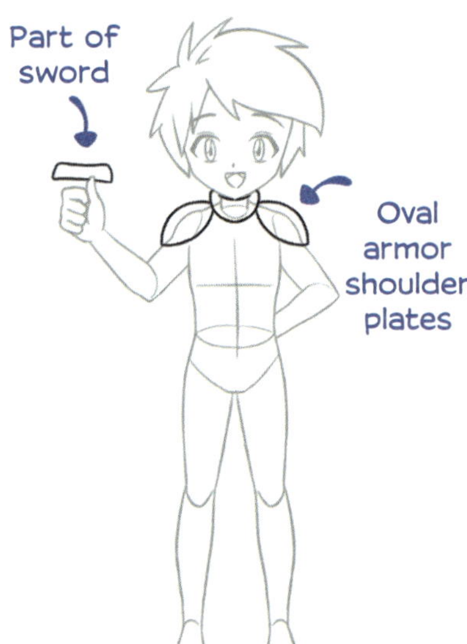

Middle line of sword blade

Follow template to trace chest and waist lines

1. Start with the neck piece and oval shoulder plates. The sword is a rectangle above the hand for now.

2. Follow the template's body and draw lines for the chest and waist. Begin the sword blade with the middle line.

3. Continue the costume down the hips in a wedge shape. Make the sword blade pointy!

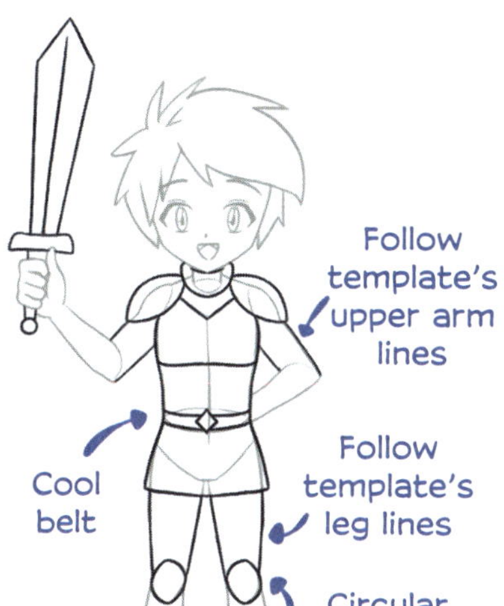

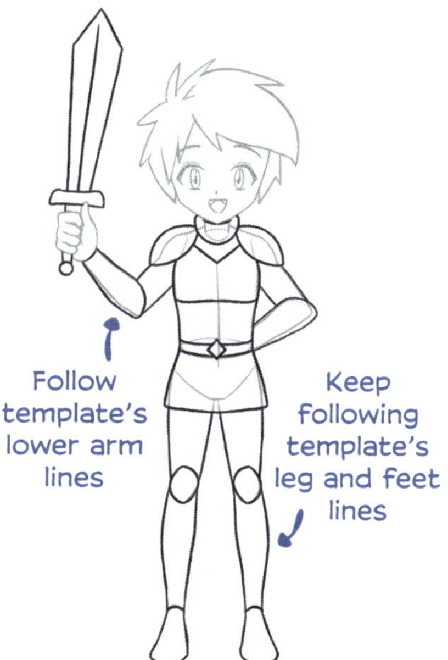

4 Trace the template's upper arms and legs. Add a cool belt, then add round knee plates to the armor.

5 Continue to follow the template's lines for the lower arms and legs.

6 Once the armor is done, give him an epic cape! It's like a big, soft triangle.

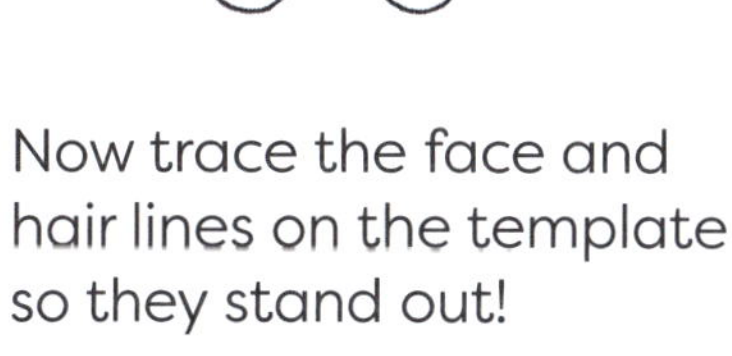

7 Now trace the face and hair lines on the template so they stand out!

LET'S COLOR!

1 Choose a skin color for his face. The rest of his body is covered.

2 Color his hair a wild color to stand out! Then fill in the cape and parts of the armor.

3 Continue with light and dark gray. For an interesting look, make his eyes different colors.

4 Add some darker blues into the hair for shadows so it looks more dimensional. Use a darker green to shade the cape, too.

Red and white creates a striking contrast.

Try browns, blues, and grays for a more muted look.

NOW YOU TRY!

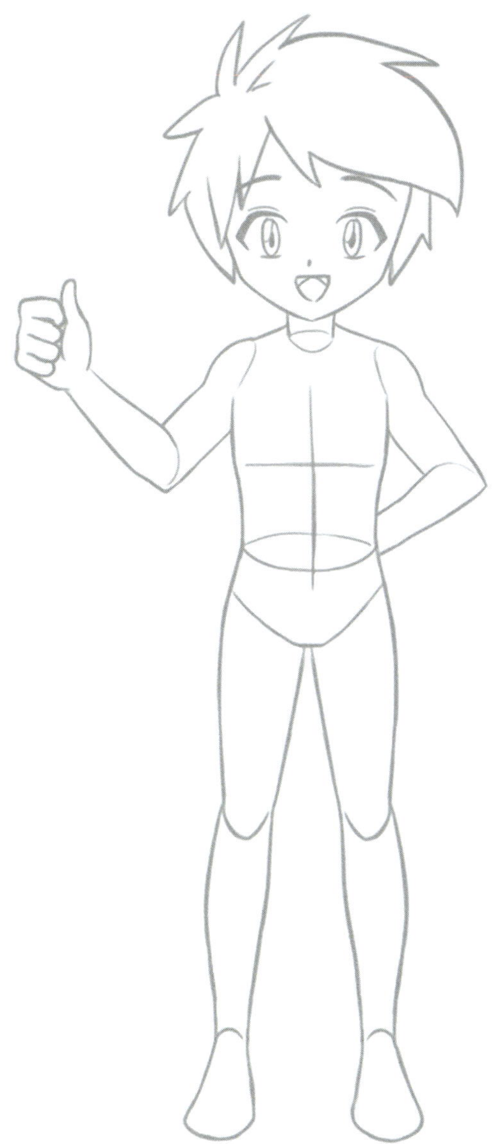

Make a photocopy of this body template, then practice drawing the clothes on it! Use the lessons in Chapter 4 to help you. There are more fun outfit ideas at the end of this chapter!

BONUS IDEAS

Now you're done with Chapter 4! Design awesome outfits on these body templates!

"I shaved half my hair with my sword!"

Basic dress shape

Note the greens are placed throughout the outfit for a harmonious look

Sporty and stylish!

"Home sweet home."

EXTRA TEMPLATES

You can photocopy these to practice as much as you want!

Here are extra body templates from Chapter 4 for you to practice drawing outfits!

Now it's time to put everything together! Combine different templates to create your own unique characters!

5

COMBINING TEMPLATES: CREATE YOUR OWN!

PUTTING IT ALL TOGETHER

This chapter is filled with fun templates for you to choose to mix together in your own unique ways!

Try these fun activities by combining templates to create your own cool characters!

You decide which templates to cut and paste together to create your own fun characters!

Photocopy the templates in this chapter. There are lots to choose from: mouths, eyes, heads, and whole bodies! Which ones will you mix together?

Decide which templates you want to combine with others. If you want, try all the ideas you have! Photocopy the templates as much as you want!

Get an adult to help you cut the templates. Be careful around scissors!

Use school glue or a glue stick to put the templates together. Now you've created a whole new character!

Turn the page for FUN examples!

IMPORTANT!

Read these SAFETY TIPS first before starting! These activities can be fun to do, but it's important to be safe at the same time!

Use safety scissors! Always ask an adult to help you cut the templates. Be aware of the sharp corners and edges of scissors—even safety scissors.

Be careful of sharp corners and edges of paper—don't poke yourself or others!

Before you begin . . .

✦ FUN ACTIVITY: EXAMPLE ONE

Try these fun activities by combining templates together in your own unique ways!

1

I photocopied the templates at the end of this example. Now I have a copy of the different head and body templates.

2

Using safety scissors carefully, I cut along the dotted lines on the templates. If you need, get an adult to cut them for you!

3

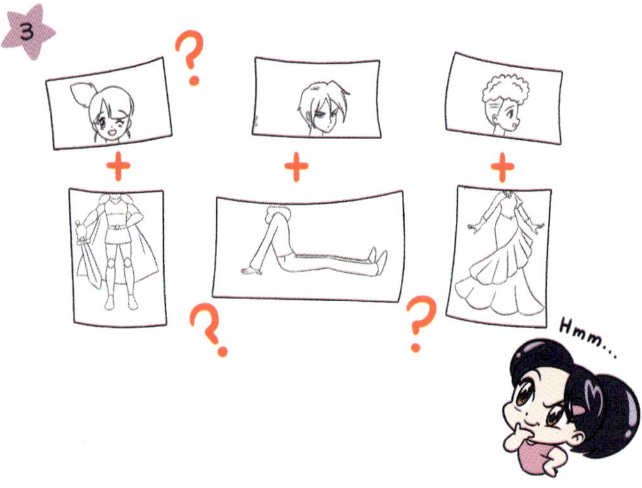

Now I have all the individual head and body templates cut. I can place them together in different combinations to see which ones I want to use to create that

4

character!
I decided which combination to make! Now, using school glue, I'll glue them together to create a new character!

There are nine different head templates and nine different body templates in this book after this example! You have lots of choices to use to create your own characters!

Sitting pretty!

Try adding your own backgrounds after!

What?! You're facing the wrong way

Try pretty, cool, silly, or just plain wacky combinations! Have fun!

EXTRA TEMPLATES

Photocopy these head and body templates, then have an adult help you cut them along the dotted lines. Combine the heads and bodies in fun ways!

Head Templates

What kinds of characters will you create?

Body Templates

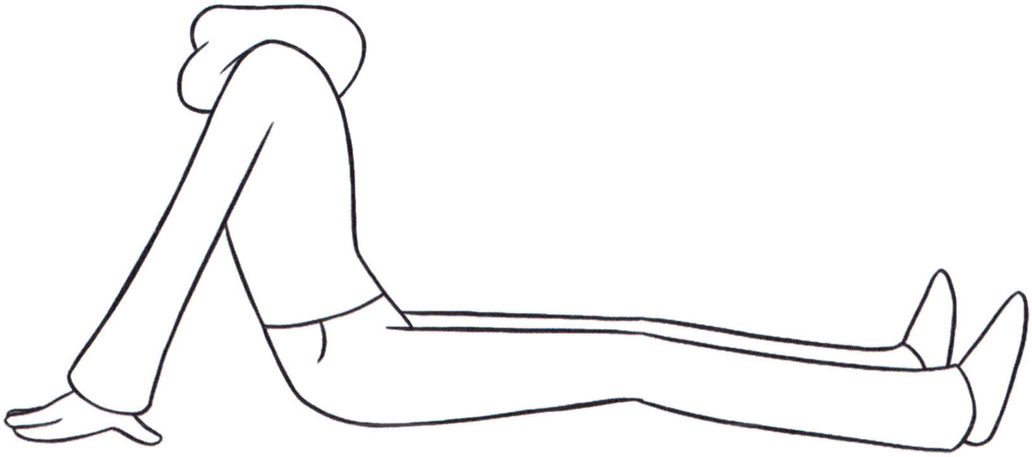

More Head Templates

More Body Templates

More Head Templates

More Body Templates

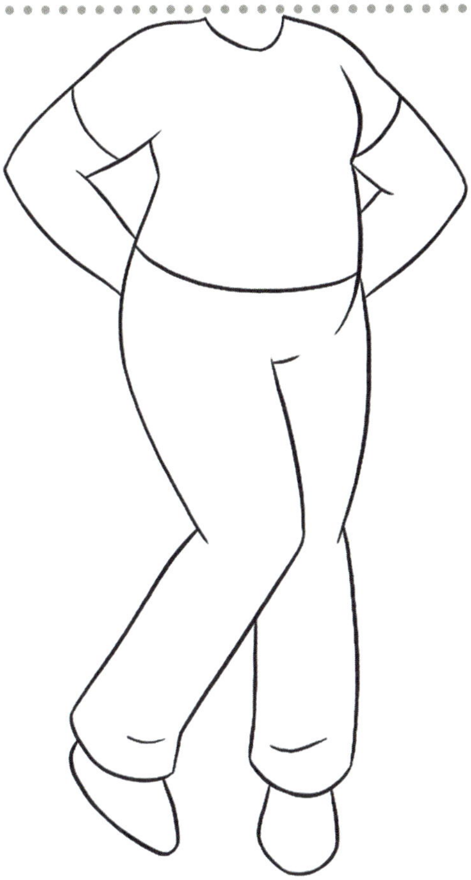

★ FUN ACTIVITY: EXAMPLE TWO

Fun eye swaps!

Try this fun activity by combining templates together in your own unique ways!

1

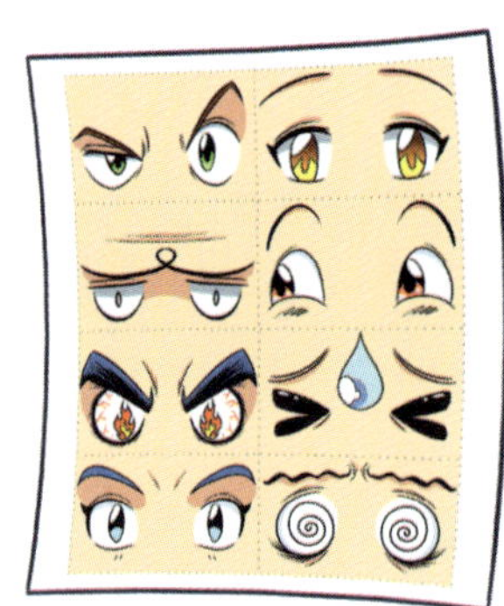

I photocopied the templates at the end of this example. Now I have a copy of the single head template and the different eyes.

2

Using safety scissors carefully, I cut along the dotted lines on the eyes templates. If you need, get an adult to cut them for you!

Now I have all the individual eyes templates cut. I can place different eyes templates on top of the head template to see which funny face I want to make!

4

I decided which combination to make! Now I'll glue the eyes template onto the face using school glue or a glue stick.

TA-DA!

OTHER IDEAS

Here are some other combinations with different eyes! What kinds of funny faces will you create?

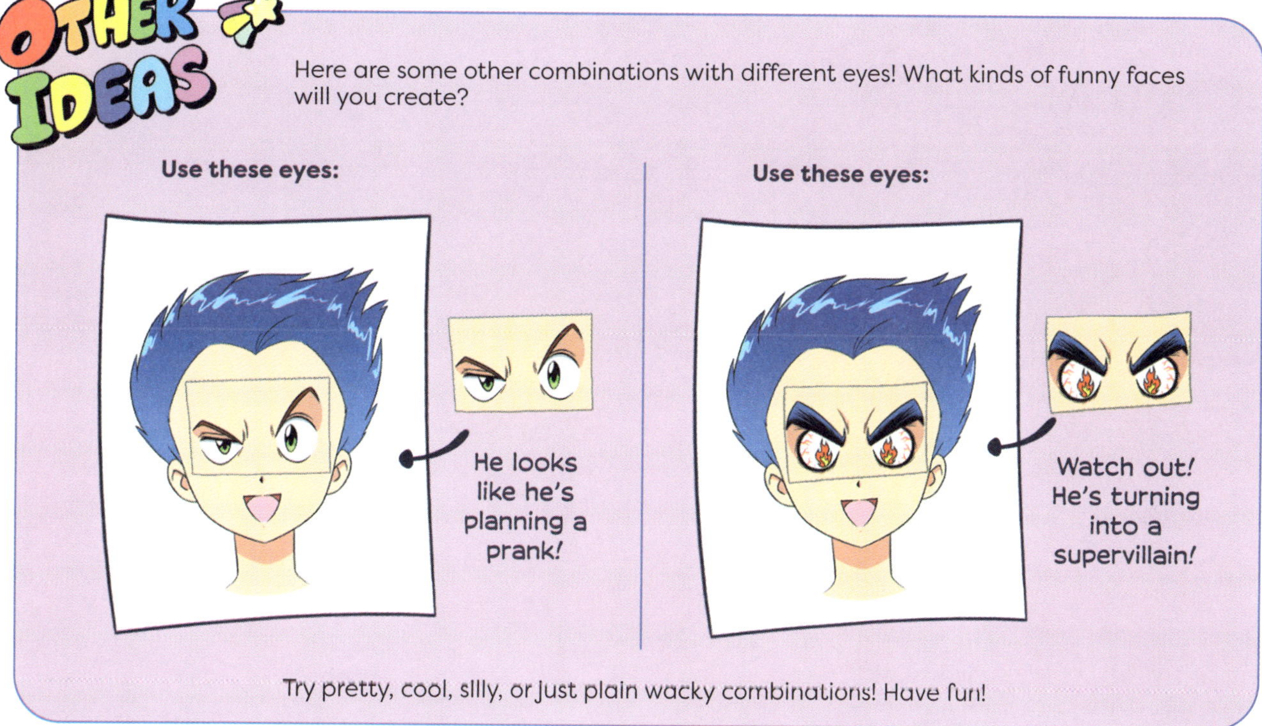

Try pretty, cool, silly, or just plain wacky combinations! Have fun!

Fun Eye Swaps!

Use the face template below and swap out the eyes from the right page to change the expression!

Photocopy the right page! Get an adult to help you cut out the pairs of eyes along the dotted lines!

Place each pair of eyes on top of the face template below to change the expression! Have fun!

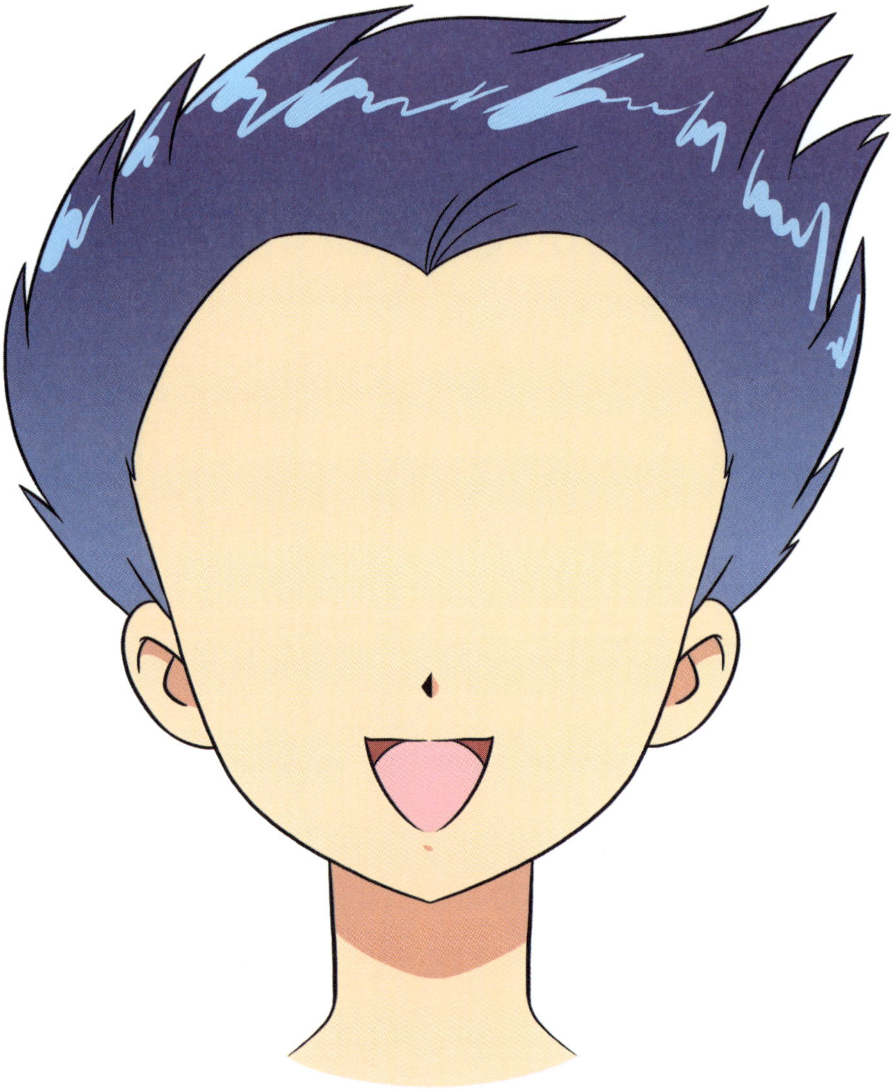

Be careful when cutting along the dotted lines!
Get an adult to help you cut the eyes out:

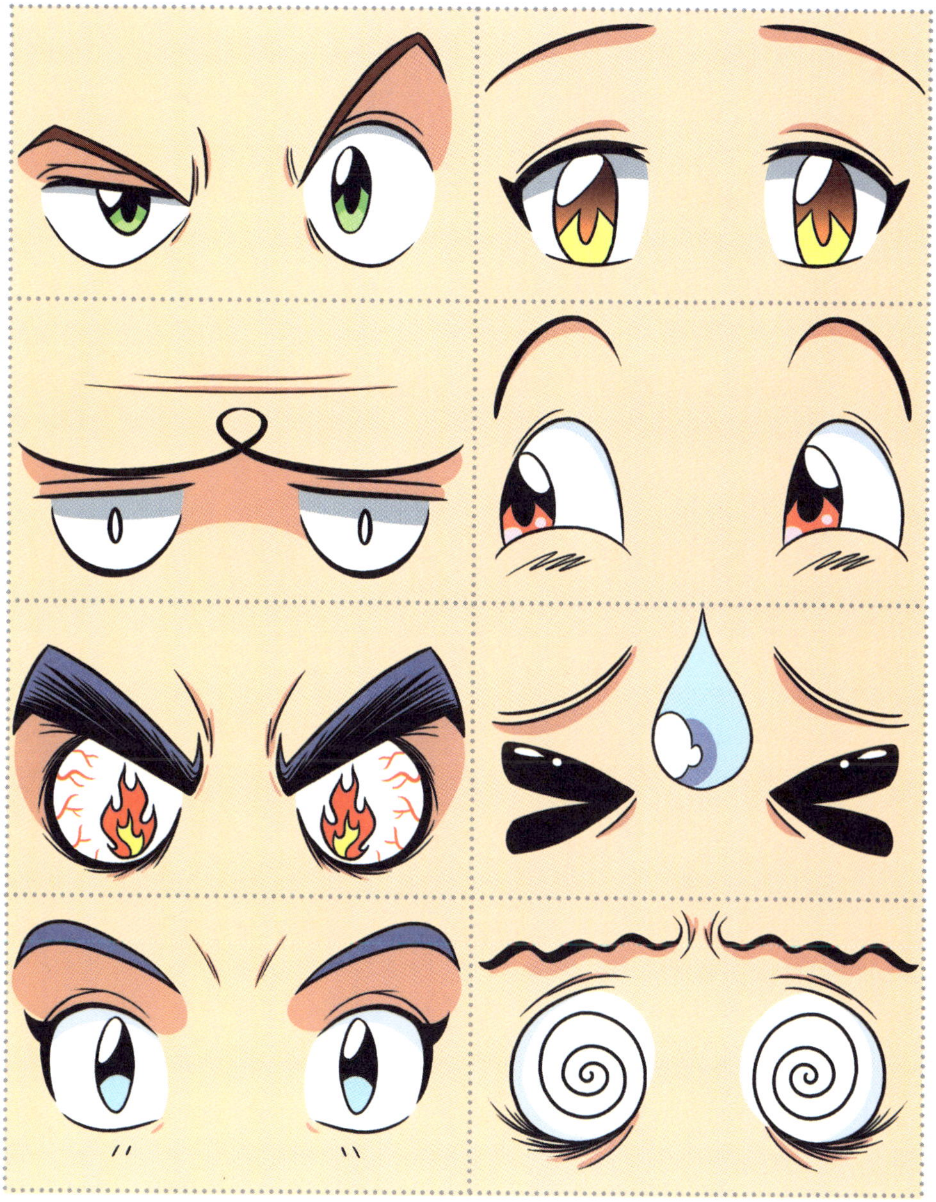

Fun Mouth Swaps!

Use the face template below and swap out the mouths from the right page to change the expression!

1 Photocopy the right page! Get an adult to help you cut out the mouths along the dotted lines!

2 Place each mouth on top of the face templates below to change the expressions! Have fun!

Be careful when cutting along the dotted lines!
Get an adult to help you cut the mouths out:

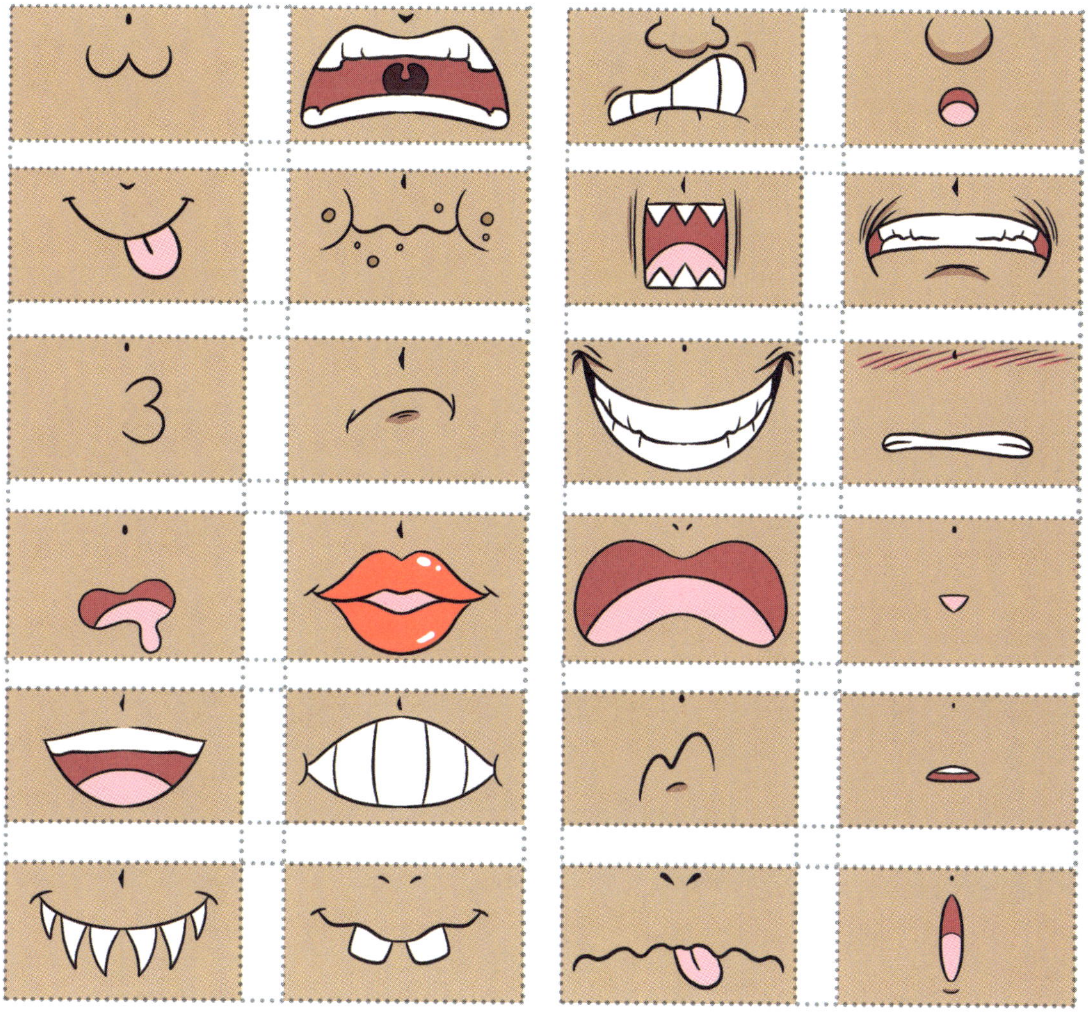

MORE BODY TEMPLATES

Photocopy these templates! Draw any head you want to go with these bodies. Make up ANY character you want. There's no right or wrong way to draw!

Use the skills you've learned from this book to create your own heads on these bodies! Go wacky, silly, cute, or cool! It's up to you!

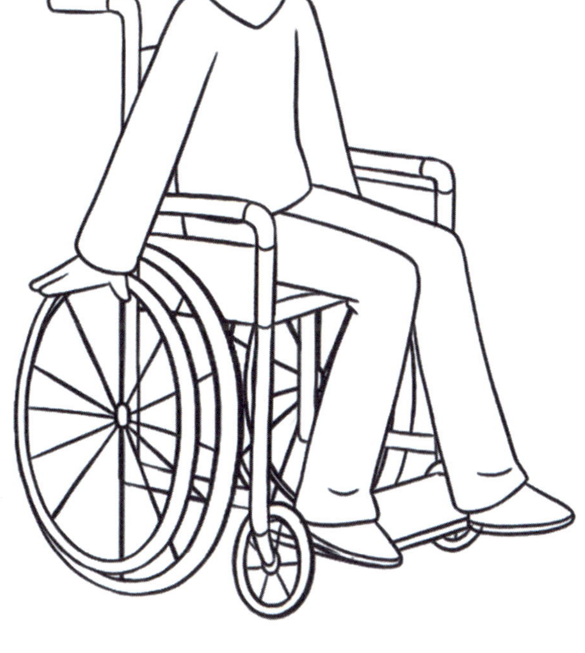

MORE HEAD TEMPLATES

Photocopy these templates! Draw any body you want to go with these heads. Make up ANY character you want. There's no right or wrong way to draw!

Photocopy these next several drawing pages, then practice drawing your own anime characters! Show your friends and family!

AUTHOR'S NOTE

I'm so glad you have my book *Draw with Mei: How to Draw Anime Characters*! I'm proud of you aspiring artists.

I hope you have fun creating your own anime characters by using the skills and templates you got from this book. If you think your drawings could be better, this is a good sign because it shows you want to improve. Just keep drawing and practicing!

Show your parents and teachers your drawings. I'm sure they'll love them!

My old childhood art

Here's how I used to draw. I'm sharing this picture with you just to show you everyone starts somewhere. Don't get discouraged. Just keep trying and keep drawing, and you will become better! I'm here cheering you on.

~ Mei

ACKNOWLEDGMENTS

I would like to send a big THANK YOU to my wonderful editor, Ardyce Alspach, whose vision, guidance, and support has been essential to the creation of this book! I'm glad to have you on my book journey, Ardyce! I would also like to thank Julie Robine for her hard work and exceptional designs in making this book stand out so beautifully! And thank you to Hayley Jozwiak and Grace House from Union Square Kids, and Steven Salpeter from Assemble Media.

To my family: Dad and Mom, thank you for buying my first sketchbook and art supplies, and for supporting my love of drawing since the very beginning! To my brother, Shawn Yu, thank you for being with me on my art journey. Without you all, I wouldn't be the artist I am today.

And thank YOU, my wonderful fans and readers from around the world!

ABOUT THE AUTHOR

Mei Yu is a multi-talented artist and author living in Vancouver. She started drawing at age two and taught herself how to draw until high school. Upon college graduation, she was immediately hired by local animation studios to do character designs for their cartoon shows. With more than 30 years of drawing experience and 20 years of teaching experience, Mei informs, entertains, and inspires her fans and readers with her books and art.

Learn more about Mei at: **meiyuart.com**